VOGUE
BEAUTY

Deborah Hutton

D0205997

HARMONY BOOKS
New York

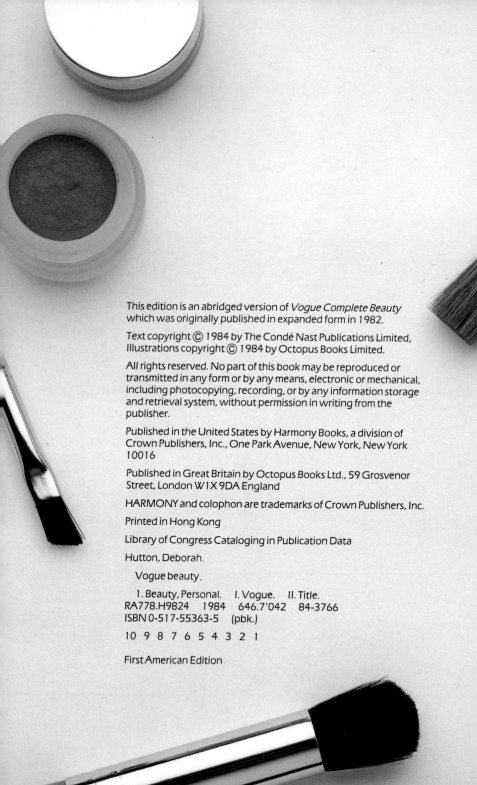

Text copyright © 1984 by The Condé Nast Publications Limited, Illustrations copyright © 1984 by Octopus Books Limited.

Published in the United States by Harmony Books, a division of Crown Publishers, Inc., One Park Avenue, New York, New York 10016

Published in Great Britain by Octopus Books Ltd., 59 Grosvenor Street, London W1X 9DA England

HARMONY and colophon are trademarks of Crown Publishers, Inc.

Printed in Hong Kong

Library of Congress Cataloging in Publication Data

Hutton, Deborah.

  Vogue beauty.

   1. Beauty, Personal.   I. Vogue.   II. Title.
RA778.H9824   1984   646.7'042   84-3766
ISBN 0-517-55363-5 (pbk.)

10 9 8 7 6 5 4 3 2 1

First American Edition

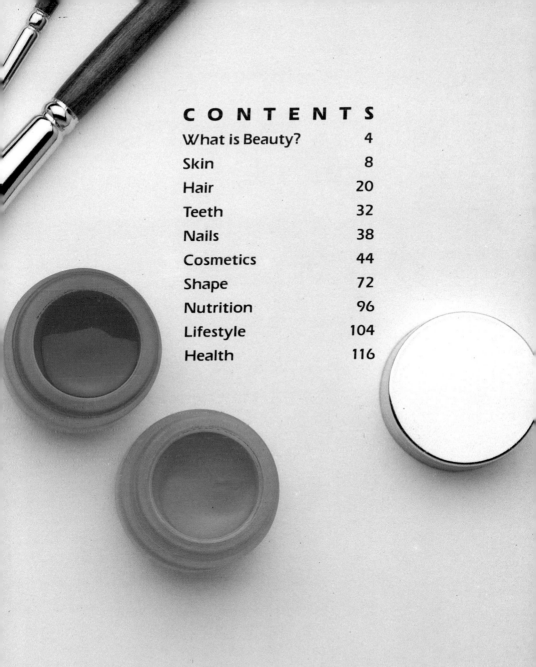

CONTENTS

what is beauty?

To the ancient Greeks, the secret of beauty lay in the proportions of the face, which they divided into three equal parts — hairline to eyebrow, eyebrow to upper lip, upper lip to chin — and called the 'Golden Section'.

Renaissance painters kept to mathematics but divided the face into seven. This was the face of the Botticelli angel, later revived by the Pre-Raphaelite artists of the late nineteenth century. Other artists, dissatisfied with both the classical and the Renaissance lineaments of physical perfection, added their own ideals. One of the most notable was Reynolds who took features from a number of sitters and reassembled them to create what he considered the perfectly beautiful face. That he could not find it for real suggests that perfection belongs to art not life and has little to do with human beauty.

The twentieth century has separated the ideal and the actual. Art has turned to the abstract — the faceless figures of Brancusi, the huge forms of Moore — leaving figurative beauty to celluloid, the relatively new media of still photography and moving film. The twentieth century also provides new insights. From 1916 onwards, *Vogue* gives an unbroken monthly commentary on how women wanted to look and who they wanted to look like. During the '30s and '40s there was a passion for imitation. Garbo, Dietrich, Hepburn…these were the originals. Many of those who followed were confections, created by film producers and publicity managers for a public that craved new idols. Looks were 'lifted', gestures copied, intonations of speech adopted. The cues came from Hollywood and their influence was enormous.

Whether women created their own idols and ideals or simply concurred with those created for them is debatable. The general inference, however, is the same… The greatest misfortune then was to be born out of one's era, with features appropriate for some undiscovered style but hopelessly inappropriate for the one of the day. 'If we can't be beauties in our period,' commiserated *Vogue*, 'let's forget it and have fun.'

While an appreciation of the idiosyncratic and unusual was still some way off, attitudes were changing. As women secured a new independence for themselves, so they were also beginning to disassociate themselves from standards of beauty set up on their behalf. Nancy Astor, quoted in *Vogue* in the 1950s, said: 'Basic beauty lies in the way a woman walks; it is health and an attitude to life'. This has a modern ring to it, for today any woman concerned about her beauty is also concerned about her health, seeing beauty not as something to be created from the outside but something to be nurtured from within.

Nancy Astor was right in recognizing that a positive outlook is important too — and that includes liking the way one looks. Too often, women become their own critics, measuring themselves against standards that do not apply and ideals that do not exist, just as surely as the arithmetically exact image created by the ancient Greeks did not exist. Too often, women turn to the mirror and are aware only of the yawning gap between what they see and what they would like to see.

If, in the future, every woman could be liberated from the apprehension of her own 'imperfections' and so freed to realize her own beauty potential, a much greater contribution would have been made to the field of beauty than any amount of new cosmetic products. For beauty not only lies in the eye of the beholder, but in the heart of the possessor. And the way to keep it there is to have a healthy regard for one's appearance and to make space for beauty in one's life, taking the time to exercise and to follow simple skincare and haircare routines, eating healthily and losing weight if necessary and revising certain aspects of lifestyle. The commitment is both to a new way of life <u>and</u> a new way of thinking. We can all have good looks provided we look after them. And looking after them depends not so much on what we failed to do yesterday or intend to do tomorrow as on what we do today ...

Today's beauty is radiant and healthy with a clear complexion, shining hair, sparkling eyes, slim figure and positive outlook – qualities epitomized by the Princess of Wales...

6

skin

1. Is your skin tone
a) even in colour and texture **b)** blotchy in colour and bumpy to the touch **c)** shiny, fairly soft and supple to the touch?

2. Are the pores on your chin and around the base of your nose visible
a) when you hold a magnifying mirror at about 15 cm (6 inches) distance **b)** only when you peer into it **c)** when you hold the mirror at arm's length?

3. Do you have a tendency to break out in spots?
a) sometimes **b)** never **c)** frequently

4. Do you have a 'break through' problem with make-up?
a) occasionally in summer; never in winter **b)** never **c)** often

5. When you sunbathe do you
a) keep your face well out of the sun or use a special sunscreen with a high SPF factor or a total sunblock **b)** use the same tanning lotion that you use for the rest of your body **c)** put nothing on your face at all – sunlight seems to help your skin?

6. How would you describe your beauty routine?
a) simple and regular **b)** elaborate **c)** erratic, obsessive or non-existent

7. When were you last aware of any change in the behaviour of your skin?
a) within the last month **b)** within the last year **c)** you have never noticed any change

8. How often do you use an exfoliant (peel-off mask, washing grains, etc) on your face?
a) regularly – once or twice a week **b)** occasionally **c)** never

Skin type: **a** answers for questions 1 to 4 indicate a fairly normal skin type; **b** a tendency to dryness and **c** a tendency to oiliness. A combination of answers? A combination skin type.

Skin care: **b** and **c** answers to questions 5 to 8 indicate that you may not be giving your skin the chance to look its best. The effects may not be immediately obvious but probably will be in 10 years' time.

Allow skin type to determine skincare routine and you will be giving your skin the best possible attention. But how much attention do you pay to your skin? Inspect your face closely in a magnifying mirror in the daylight. Then complete the questionnaire.

The type of skin you have is determined by two unalterables — your genes and your sex — governed by your age and affected by the environment. It can also be enormously improved by the way you look after it. Skincare today means thinking 10, 20 and even 50 years ahead, protecting yourself against the harmful effects of sunlight, pollution and stress and having the wisdom to take the best from science and the natural world.

The largest and one of the most remarkable organs of the body, your skin provides a most accurate key to its inner state of health because it is a dynamic structure, continually renewing itself and constantly changing in response to many external and internal stimuli. It regulates body temperature by adjusting the rate of water elimination — sweat. It insulates the body from the cold by means of a primitive response that causes the fine hairs to stand on end — goose pimples. It frees the system from accumulated toxins and metabolic waste and can be one of the first and most immediate aids to diagnosis in the event of illness, such as diabetes, anaemia and diseases of the liver, kidneys and bile duct. Finally, it acts in a protective capacity, keeping your insides in, and harmful substances in the atmosphere out. Very few substances are actually absorbed through the skin: it is a powerful barrier to many of the potential hazards with which you daily come into contact — ultraviolet radiation, for example.

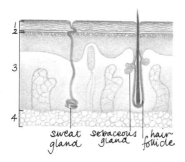

sweat gland   sebaceous gland   hair follicle

The skin comprises several layers. The epidermis (1) is composed of dead skin cells which protect the young live cells beneath. These originate in the basal layer (2) and gradually travel upwards. Damage at basal level may disrupt genetic pattern and result in scarring. The dermis (3) is composed of tough connective tissue. A layer of fat (4) gives the skin a springy texture.

When out sunbathing, assess your risk of burning by using your body as a sundial. Lie down on the sand or the ground and mark out two lines where your head and feet reach. Stand at one end so that your shadow slopes towards the other. If it falls short of the mark, the sun is especially burning and you should be extremely careful.

If tanning as fast as possible without burning is your only consideration when choosing a sun cream, think again. You could be taking a short and sure route to a prematurely aged skin and significantly increasing the risk of getting skin cancer, developing a cataract or disrupting your immune system.

Sunlight damages skin because the ultraviolet strikes at the nucleus of the skin cell, altering the DNA (the genetic code) and preventing it from renewing itself perfectly. Although we can all escape fairly lightly with a small amount of sun exposure, intensive sunbathing over the years will cause cells to divide more and more defectively and the damage to become increasingly visible.

Sunlight is important for the health of mind and body, potentially dangerous for the skin. Capitalize on the benefits and safeguard yourself against the dangers with a good, broad spectrum, water-resistant sun cream for the body (see chart, below, to identify your skin type and the sun protection factor you should be using) and a total sunblock or high protection factor sunscreen (10 or above) for the face and neck.

SUN PROTECTION FACTORS: which should you be using?

Skin type	Very strong sun		Less strong sun		Skin's natural protection
	Untanned	Tanned	Untanned	Tanned	
Ultra-sensitive (always burns, never tans)	12	8	8	6	5/10 minutes
Very sensitive (often burns, rarely tans)	8	6	6	4	10/20 minutes
Averagely sensitive (burns then tans)	6	4	4	3/2	20/30 minutes
Less sensitive (rarely burns, tans easily and deeply)	4	3/2	3/2	3/2	40 minutes

Washing and Cleansing

Do not disturb the skin's normal function any more than you have to. Left to itself, the skin is a remarkable, self-cleansing and self-nourishing organ — and both nourishing and cleansing come from the inside. The purpose of washing is to take off surface grime and excess oil regularly and efficiently, but never abrasively.

Because the skin is constantly changing in response to different stimuli, what is right one week may not always be appropriate the next. Pay attention to your skin. If it feels dry and taut, you may be treating it too harshly, using over-strong products or exposing it to unreasonable amounts of sun and wind. If it is shiny and oily with a tendency to break out, ask yourself whether you are removing every trace of greasy make-up removers, whether you would be better off washing it with soap and water or whether, perhaps, you are over-washing it. If your skin develops lumps, bumps, pimples or scaly patches, simplify cleansing and make-up routines. Wash or cleanse the skin once a day only, using mild, unscented soaps and lotions

Wash the face with a mild unperfumed soap, lather briefly and rinse thoroughly. If the skin feels dry and tight after washing, try using a superfatted soap which incorporates emollients such as lanolin or mineral oil into the soap base. Other causes of dryness: over-washing, incomplete rinsing, hard water (calcium and magnesium salts in the water combine with the soap to form a drying 'scum' on the skin) or sensitivity. Try a cream cleanser instead.

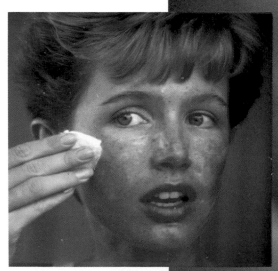

washwashwash

Take as much care removing make-up as putting it on. Incompletely removed particles may block pores and contribute to skin problems, while flaking mascara or eye make-up can irritate eyes. Start by tying hair well back from face. If you wear contact lenses, remove these now.

cleansecleanse

Skim a light liquid make-up remover over face and lips, around the eyes and down the neck as far as you have taken the foundation. Leave make-up and remove on the face for a few moments, to help the make-up dissolve. Take a folded tissue or a piece of cotton wool and wipe it ov the face and neck in an upwards and outwards direction.

Most face foundations, blushers, powders and make-up bases are water-soluble and can usually be efficiently removed with soap and water. If particles of make-up still cling to the face or come away on the cotton wool you are using for toning, use a cleanser. If you have an oily skin, choose one that flows easily from the bottle, is well absorbed by cotton wool and leaves no shiny residue on the skin surface. A drier skin will benefit from a slightly

Eyes need special attention. The skin is very delicate here and the eyes are susceptible to irritation, even infection, if make-up or make-up remover come too close. Use a specially formulated, water-soluble lotion so that any make-up entering the eye can be easily flushed out by the tear fluid.

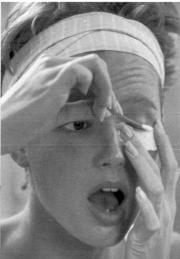

Wipe off with a piece of dampened cotton wool to prevent stray particles or fibres getting caught on the lashes or irritating the eye. Use a cotton wool bud around the immediate margins of the eye. Finally, wipe any traces of eye make-up or mascara away from the eyes, use a toner to remove any traces of greasiness left by the cleanser and follow with a light moisturizer.

When removing mascara, attend to lower and upper lashes, underneath as well as on top. Place a moistened tissue underneath the lower lashes, then smooth a small amount of the cleanser on to a cotton wool bud and roll it over top and lower lashes together.

heavier cream. Both types, however, should avoid the heavier, greasepaint type of remover. Theatrical make-up belongs to the theatre, so if you need a heavy cream to get your make-up off at night, it is time to rethink your make-up techniques.

To take make-up off: use gentle sweeping movements and continue with successive pieces of cotton wool until the last comes away clean.

Toning

Skin toners have an evaporating and cooling action that causes muscles to contract and pores to become temporarily (not permanently) smaller. Toning is pleasant and refreshing, and is valuable in removing traces of grease the cleanser may have left behind.

Products are generally divided into fresheners, toners, clarifying lotions and astringents. Fresheners are the mildest, toners and clarifying lotions tend to be more abrasive, while astringents are the harshest of the lot. You can make your own toner by mixing witch hazel, which has strong astringent properties, with gentler rosewater. Use equal quantities for oily skins, two parts of rosewater to one of witch hazel for normal skins, and the same mixture diluted with distilled water if the skin is really dry. Bottle and keep in the refrigerator.

Straight witch hazel also makes an excellent 'emergency' treatment for spots and pimples.

Cells that have been too long on the surface of the skin are greyish and dull in tone, may flake and can clog the sebaceous pores, leading to superficial spots or blackheads. Cosmetic exfoliation helps speed up the shedding process by taking off the uppermost, dead layer of cells to expose the finer, more translucent tissue underneath.

Moisturizing

Moisturizers work by duplicating and strengthening the role of the body's own, naturally produced sebum and thus protect the skin against excessive moisture loss. Significantly, many moisturizers contain lanolin, which is derived from the natural oil (sebum) of the sheep. Like the oil on the skin's surface, moisturizers are water-and-oil emulsions. If you have a very dry skin, use an oil-based emulsion; if a normal or combination skin a lighter, water-based lotion. How can you tell the difference? Oil-based emulsions are thicker, are not absorbed as well and leave a fine reflective sheen on the skin.

Exfoliating

Cosmetic exfoliation may help preserve the youthful bloom of the skin. Some dermatologists maintain that the reason men's skin lines less rapidly around the mouth and cheeks than women's is because the practice of shaving every day acts as a natural exfoliant.

Cosmetic exfoliation can be accomplished in a number of ways. The ancient Egyptians used a recipe containing alabaster, honey and oatmeal and you can make up your own by combining roasted oatmeal with the zest of a citrus fruit and mixing to a paste with a little water. Alternatively, you can use one of the commercial brands, a rough face glove or rotating facial 'scrubbing' brush, a peel-off mask or a chemical solution which usually contains a 'grease-stripping' agent, such as salicylic acid, resorcinol or benzoyl peroxide.

Whichever method you use, always exfoliate according to your skin's strength. The purpose is to leave the skin glowing, not inflamed and irritated. Use with caution on dry and sensitive faces, but tougher body skin can well withstand a vigorous, twice-weekly sloughing session to encourage the skin to flake off and to boost circulation. Special attention areas: 'gooseflesh' on upper arms, thighs and buttocks and rough patches on knees and elbows. Follow with body lotion.

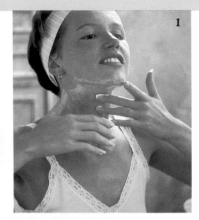

1

2

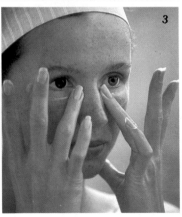

3

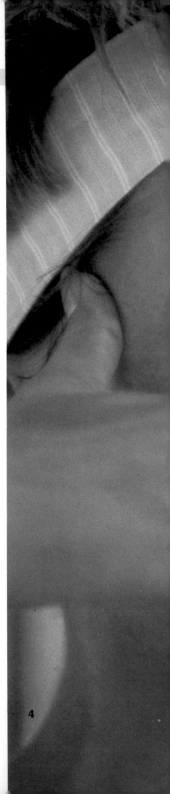

4

A good facial massage will relax you and invigorate your skin by boosting the circulation and dilating the blood vessels, bringing more oxygen to the skin surface. Use a light moisturizer if skin is oily, a richer night cream if dry, and smooth it onto face and neck.

Start at the collarbone. Brush fingers up the neck and out under the chin (1). Use the backs of the fingers, too, if you like. Tap fingertips all around the mouth and chin. Give a deeper massage on the cheeks. Hold the fingers as though grasping an invisible ball and let the knuckles of the fingers play over the cheeks (2). Roll the skin gently between the first and second fingers and continue until the skin tingles.

'Anchor' thumbs under chin to ensure the lightest touch when massaging eyes. Starting at inner corners, smooth fourth finger up over browbone, down below the eyes and into the corners again (3). Leave a fairly wide margin around the eye. Relieve any underlying tension by placing first and second fingers firmly on the temples and pressing down. Finish with a firm upward stroke along bridge of nose and forehead. Place thumbs on temples for stability and bring hands up alternately (4), concentrating the pressure on the outer edge of the first finger. Imagine all the creases being smoothed away. Continue until you feel completely relaxed.

hair

1. Which best describes the texture of your hair?
a) fine and straight **b)** neither fine nor coarse and slightly wavy
c) coarse and wavy or curly **d)** none of the above

2. Which best describes the colour of your hair?
a) fair or mouse **b)** dark **c)** red, auburn or grey

3. Which best describes the condition of your hair?
a) shiny but lank **b)** glossy **c)** dull and frizzy

4. Three days after washing, how does your hair look?
a) oily and limp **b)** ready for a wash **c)** shinier and more
manageable than after washing **d)** OK, but scalp would feel itchy

**5. Do you use heated rollers, curling tongs or hot hair dryer
when drying your hair?**
a) yes, frequently **b)** yes, occasionally **c)** never

6. Have you had any of the following done in the last year?
a) highlights, temporary or semi-permanent tints **b)** bleaching at
the salon or in the sunlight, perming or straightening, permanent
tint (does not include 'natural' dyes such as henna) **c)** none of these

7. Does your hair lose its texture when wet?
a) no **b)** yes, it becomes very matted and limp like wet cotton wool

8. Scrape the scalp gently with a comb. Is there any scaling?
a) yes, small white flakes **b)** yes, larger scales **c)** no

**9. If yes to 8a or b, do any of the following apply? Skin is
generally dry; you have been away to a hot climate; you rinse
hair once only after shampooing; you use hair sprays and/or
setting lotions; you suffer from psoriasis or eczema?**
a) yes **b)** no

Hair type: **a** answers to questions 1-4 indicate hair is oily; **b** that it is
normal or mixed condition (dry at the ends, oily on the scalp –
particularly likely if yes to **4d**), **c** that it is dry either through lack of
proper care (**5a**) or chemical processing (**6b**). This is particularly
likely if your hair is porous (**7b**).

Scalp condition: If you answered **8a** or **b**, you could have a flaking
scalp condition – not necessarily dandruff. Positive answers to **9**
indicate other culprits.

Your hair condition owes
much more to what you do to
it than to what nature, in
terms of genetic inheritance,
does to you. But how well do
you look after it?

Your hair should be your crowning glory. Not only is it the first thing that people notice about you but it also offers the most immediate prospect of change that you have. Change your cut, experiment with colour and you can spell out a whole new look.

Because there are no rules about the way you should wear your hair, advice on cut is not given. Your hairdresser will be able to match up a style compatible with your hair type, face shape and personality in a way no book can do. Guidelines on colour are given, however, together with a chart so that you can check out each process against the present colour and condition of your hair and arrive at one that will work well for you.

Caring for the scalp

You cannot get the best from your hair if you do not have a healthy scalp. But do not automatically assume a scaling scalp means dandruff. It could indicate a dry skin which should be treated with a light almond oil massage; too much sun causing the scalp to burn and peel; or, commonly, a residue left in the hair after shampooing or using a hair spray or setting lotion. Consider these first and, if your scalp does not respond, treat it with a weak cetrimide solution, made by gently heating half a teaspoon of the powder in 1.2 litres/2 pints (5 cups) of distilled water until completely dissolved. Part the hair at 2 cm (½ inch) intervals and apply to the scalp with swabs of cotton wool. If the condition continues, switch to an anti-dandruff shampoo containing tar or zinc pyrithione, which has a slowing effect on the rate of cell turnover.

Massaging the scalp can have several benefits. Arch the hands into a dome shape and use the pads of the fingers in a firm, circular movement, rather as though you were kneading dough. Keep the scalp damp by dipping your fingers into plain tapwater for normal hair and scalp; cetrimide solution for dandruffed and scaly scalps; the juice of half a lemon in a cupful of water for oily and mixed condition hair; warm almond oil for dry scalp and hair.

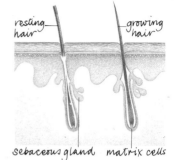

resting hair — growing hair

sebaceous gland   matrix cells

Hair grows from a cluster of matrix cells beneath the skin. These cells divide rapidly and push the new hair up towards the scalp. When the new hair emerges at the scalp it is effectively keratinized (dead). The sebaceous glands at the side of the hair follicle are largely responsible for the lustre of the hair: too much sebum will produce an oily hair condition; too little a dry one. Each hair observes a growing phase (above), a resting phase of between two or three months (left) and a falling out phase. By the time the old hair is shed a new one will have already begun to form beneath it.

To check the condition of your scalp, make a parting down the centre of your head and scrape it gently with a wide-toothed comb (right). If there is any scaling, your scalp needs attention – but consult the checklist of possible culprits, left, before you assume it is dandruff.

	CAUSES	TREATMENT
OILY	Overactive sebaceous glands. All hair tends to become greasier at puberty when the sebaceous glands become much more active due to hormonal changes. In some cases it can also become noticeably oilier at times of smaller hormonal fluctuation, such as before menstruation. Oily hair usually improves during the last six months of pregnancy when there is a surge in several hormones.	Keep scrupulously clean and wash daily with a mild shampoo. This will not step up sebaceous gland activity, but harsh-acting shampoos will. Avoid 'dry' shampoos (powder can clog the hair follicles on the scalp and aggravate the problem). Add the juice of half a lemon or one tablespoon of vinegar to a jugful of water and use it as a final rinse. Use lower heat settings on blow dryers. Hot air currents can activate the sweat glands, step up sebum production. As processing tends to dry out moisture within hair, mild colouring (not bleaching) can improve the appearance of oily hair.
NORMAL	Healthy-looking, shining hair is the result of well-balanced internal chemistry (good genetic profile and well-regulated hormone levels), common sense and careful management.	Wash your hair as often as you think it needs it – every day if necessary, using a shampoo and a conditioner that suits you, and interfering with its natural function as little as possible. Use colouring processes with caution.

	CAUSES	TREATMENT
DRY	Four to 13 per cent of healthy hair is water. Dry hair is usually symptomatic of dehydration, often caused by a lack of sebum. Dry hair not only looks dull and lifeless, but is also much more susceptible to breakage and splitting due to its reduced elasticity. Take steps to protect it from stresses, such as brushing, pulling or harsh styling. As strong sunlight exerts a natural and damaging bleaching effect, protect hair by wearing a scarf or wide-brimmed hat in hot weather.	Shampoo once only with a mild shampoo. If you massage scalp thoroughly, the hair will be cleaned effectively. Use a good cream conditioner, rinse thoroughly and keep brushing or combing to a minimum when wet. If the hair is very dry, massage two tablespoons of warmed olive or almond oil well into the hair and leave for at least 30 minutes. Remove oil by pouring shampoo directly onto the head, massaging well and rinsing. Finger dry or leave to dry in the open air, if possible. Hair dryers should be used with care. Most dry hair is inflicted, not inherited – and colouring, perming or straightening and bleaching (in ascending order of severity) are the principal culprits. Either avoid processing and wait for condition to improve or go for highlights or one of the milder colouring processes.
MIXED CONDITION	Active sebaceous glands produce a glut of sebum that is absorbed at the base of the scalp and prevented from travelling along the hair shaft, robbing it of essential lubrication and gloss. Hence, the scalp and hair at the roots are oily, while the ends are dry, frizzy and prone to breakage and splitting.	Discriminate between cleansing scalp and ends of the hair. Each qualifies for separate attention. Give scalp an astringent treatment before shampooing (see previous page), follow with a mild shampoo, used once only. Finish with a conditioner on the ends only. Use lowest setting when blow drying and follow colouring guidelines for dry hair.

washwash

Washing

Wet hair loses up to 20 per cent of its natural elasticity, making it an easy and vulnerable target to over-vigorous shampooing and drying. Most people do more damage to their hair through insensitive washing and drying than through using the 'wrong' shampoos. Shampoos, however, are popular scapegoats.

Choosing the right shampoo is largely a matter of trial and error, unless you are already using a prescription treatment specially made up for you by a trichologist. When choosing shampoo, do not be blinded by protein, promises or pH numbérs. Go by what suits you. A good shampoo should clean quickly and effectively, should be easy to apply and to rinse out and should never irritate the scalp. Do not judge the effectiveness of any given shampoo by the lather it produces. Some manufacturers add foaming agents for purely commercial reasons.

Wet hair loses up to 20 per cent of its elasticity and, with it, much of its natural resilience. So treat it as gently as possible after washing.

- Squeeze out excess water, wrap hair loosely in a clean towel, turban-fashion, and press firmly against the head. Do not rub vigorously.
- Once hair is no longer soaking wet, the best thing you can do is to leave it to dry naturally.
- When using a blow dryer, capitalize on the control, minimize on the damage: do not start drying until the hair is three-quarters dry; do not hold the dryer over one area of the head for too long; do not allow the scalp to become hot; use a brush gently to persuade the hair into the style you want; and, most important, do not continue to blow hot air on to hair that is already dry.

27

NATURAL (VEGETABLE) DYES

Dye	Best effects on
Henna	All shades of brown and black. On the whole, the darker the tone, the more effective the result. Not recommended by those with grey or fair hair as it can look very carroty. Lasts permanently (henna is even more irremovable than a blue/black tint); roots need retouching every six to eight weeks.
Chamomile	Naturally blonde hair (very subtle bleaching effect). Chamomile will also brighten darker hair; combined with red wine, it will give a warm glow to light/medium brown hair. Lasts as above.

To use

Wearing rubber gloves, apply paste first to the ends of the hair within an inch of the scalp and then to the roots where the colour develops much more quickly. Cover with plastic or foil and leave for about 35 minutes. Then check the colour by testing a strand of hair. DO NOT APPLY HEAT: this will affect the final colour. shampoo and rinse out thoroughly.

Brew like tea, using 25 g/1 oz chamomile flower heads per 600 ml/1 pint (2½ cups) of boiling water; leave to infuse for 20 minutes and pour over the hair several times as a final rinse. Alternatively, boil 25 g/1 oz quassia chips in a little water for 30 minutes, pour over 25 g/1 oz ground chamomile and apply as a paste like henna (see above). Dry naturally.

CHEMICAL DYES

Dye	Best effects on
Temporary rinses	Light, mousy or greying hair. Lasts until next wash.
Metallic 'crazy' colour sprays	Lighter shades. Will last visibly until brushed or washed off – though an invisible deposit of the metallic substance may still remain; see right.
Semi-permanent rinses	Light to medium brown hair, giving a darker, richer glint; lightish grey or white hair to give darker cover. Will last for four to six shampoos.
Permanent tints	Any colour. Lasts permanently; regrowth tint on the roots necessary at four to six weekly intervals.
Highlights/ lowlights	Dark mousy blondes – though they can look good on almost any type of hair, including brown, red and grey. If you have brown or red hair, subtle chestnut or marmalade tones can look sensational. Lasts permanently; roots will need retouching after three to four months.

To use

After shampooing; as directed on packet. Do not over-apply or the hair will become dull.

As directed; protect your eyes when spraying.
NB Never tint hair if you have used any metallic preparation on it without first asking your hairdresser to do a strand test.

After shampooing, leave for between 20 and 40 minutes, depending on intensity of tone required, and rinse out. Semi-permanent colours will not add or change colour; they will intensify colour already present; not recommended for fair hair. Patch test before using.

Strictly as directed on the packet. Never on eyelashes, eyebrows or hair elsewhere on the body. Preferably not when pregnant. Patch test for allergies, if doing it yourself.

Section off hair with clips and brush fine strands with the lightening solution (back of head first, around hairline and crown last, where the colour develops more quickly). Wrap strands in silver foil to make neat parcels. Watch timing carefully and rinse thoroughly. NB It is really advisable to go to a professional colorist to have highlights put in.

REMOVING UNWANTED HAIR

Method	Where and when not to use
Shaving	Never on the face, around the nipples or the bikini line, where the angles are difficult to get right and there is a strong risk of cutting yourself.
Tweezing/ Plucking	Only pluck the eyebrows. Tweezing is the greatest stimulator of hair growth because it can activate a repair hormone which induces increased cell production within the hair follicle.
Depilatory Creams	Almost anywhere except eyebrows, breasts and face, unless the label stipulates that it is safe. Always take especial care around the bikini line. Patch test first, following the maker's instructions. If no reaction in 24 hours, apply it.
Waxing (profes- sionally)	Never on painful, inflamed or sunburned skin; the nipples or the face.
Waxing (at home)	As above.
Bleaching	Always use a bleach specially formulated for the face and avoid commercial hair bleaches which may turn the hair yellow. If hair does not respond within the time allowed, consider electrolysis.
Electrolysis (profes- sionally)	Never in the inner ear and nostrils, on eyelashes, moles or warts, on or around the nipple if pregnant or breastfeeding and anywhere where the skin is infected, inflamed or unevenly pigmented. Avoid electrolysis if you are a diabetic and your doctor advises against it or if you have an allergy to metals. Go to a reputable and properly qualified electrolysist. Incorrect treatment can lead to infection or scarring.

Description

Shaving is quick, easy and efficient and does not cause the hair to grow back thicker or darker although the regrowth feels rougher because the hairs have been cut square. To shave: use soap and water to help razor glide over skin. Always shave in the direction of hair growth to avoid ingrown hairs.

Works best when there are only a few hairs to remove. Always pluck hair in a good light, with a magnifying mirror and in the direction of hair growth. Pluck one at a time from the underneath of the eyebrow only.

These dissolve the protein structure that gives the hair its strength and texture. The destructive action of the chemical is limited by how far the cream can penetrate. When using, always follow maker's instructions and time yourself carefully. If cream does not work effectively within the time stated, use another method instead.

1. HOT wax is applied in patches, allowed to cool and stripped off taking the hairs with it. Hair is removed from deepest possible point – just above the root. This method can irrritate a sensitive skin.
2. COLD wax is smoothed over the area and covered with gauze, which is then stripped away taking wax and hairs with it. Cold wax is not as harsh on skin, and so better if very sensitive, but it is not as effective for removing very thick or coarse hair.

1. HOT waxes are much trickier but give better results. Make sure your kit includes an in-built thermostat control. Apply wax according to instructions, and wait for it to set like toffee. Do not let it become brittle. Remove against direction of hair growth. If wax hardens, apply another layer and pull them both off together.
2. COLD pre-waxed strips are more manageable and quicker, but not as effective. In cold weather, place them on a radiator to soften.

Bleaching is an excellent way of dealing with dark hair on the face (and on the legs if you are going out into the sun). Although it can be done professionally, the home kits are so good that results are equally impressive. The effect can often last up to four weeks.

Electrolysis is the only widely used way of removing hair permanently. It uses an electric current (shortwave diathermy) to kill the hair and only the most sensitive of skins will find it painful. It is uncomfortable, however. A newer method uses tweezers to pass the current through the hair shaft, but this is not as effective.
    Not all the hairs will be killed the first time but, while some do grow back, the hair will be finer and the shaft weaker and less resilient with each regrowth – though it can take as long as 18 months to clear a lipline. (Home kits are not recommended.)

teeth

1. When did you last see your dentist?
a) within the last six months **b)** within the last year **c)** you cannot remember

2. Have you ever been shown how to brush your teeth properly and how to look after your mouth?
a) yes **b)** no

3. When did you last have your teeth professionally cleaned and polished?
a) within six months **b)** in the last year **c)** more than a year ago

4. Do you use plaque-disclosing tablets?
a) regularly **b)** rarely **c)** never

5. What happens when you use dental floss?
a) it slides easily up and down between the teeth once past the point where they meet **b)** it gets caught and snagged **c)** you never use it

6. With regular (twice daily) brushing, how long does a toothbrush last before the bristles splay out?
a) about three months **b)** one to three months **c)** less than a month

7. Look carefully at your gums in a mirror. Note how they look. Then clean them thoroughly and inspect them carefully again. Are they
a) the same colour as before and lying fairly flat against teeth
b) reddish, slightly inflamed and/or bleeding a little, especially at the gum/tooth margin **c)** very sore, inflamed and/or bleeding profusely?

8. How often do you clean your teeth?
a) twice a day **b)** once a day **c)** erratically, whenever you remember

All these questions are designed to help you test the relative health of your teeth and gums – in themselves a reflection of how well you are looking after them. If you scored all **a** answers, congratulations – you are one of two per cent of the population with no signs of gum disease, a healthy mouth and an efficient teeth cleaning method. If you scored any **b** and **c** answers, read on to see how your current teeth cleaning routine might be improved. If you answered **1b, c, 2b** and **3c**, make an appointment to see your dentist or dental hygienist.

If your teeth cleaning routine is thorough, your mouth will be healthy. If dental hygiene is lax, your gums will be infected and your teeth may be in jeopardy. How well do you look after them?

To brush teeth: start at back of outer side of lower jaw. Hold brush at 45 degrees, so that bristles nudge just under fold of gum. Now, gently flex bristles back and forth. Repeat all way round then attend to inner side and, finally, upper jaw, It is essential to treat upper and lower teeth independently. Scrub biting surfaces. Flossing is important because no tooth brushing routine, however efficient, can clean more than three of the five sides of the tooth. Wrap floss around the tooth in a wide V-shape. Slide it down just a little way into the gum crevice and up again.

We are not all born with the potential for perfect teeth, but heredity is a popular scapegoat for bad teeth and an unhealthy mouth. Conversely, good teeth and a healthy mouth can be acquired by almost anyone, provided that the battle against tooth decay and gum disease is started early, that the teeth are straightened or rearranged (if necessary), and that they are looked after well. Teeth fall out for specific and preventable reasons and age is not one of them. In fact, it has been estimated that a healthy tooth will outlast its owner by some 200 years.

Looking after your teeth
The acid responsible for producing decay is a by-product of the sucrose in refined carbohydrates. Painless in the early stages, decay attacks the outer edges of the enamel before spreading into the soft, sensitive dentine beneath. As all sticky, sugary foods can cause decay they should be avoided as much as possible.

A tenacious and transparent plaque film forms from

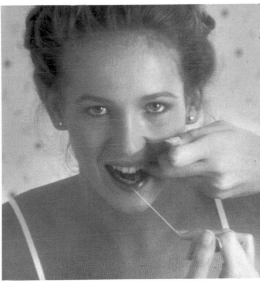

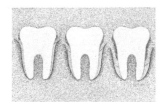

After the age of 16, more teeth are lost through gum disease than decay. The insidious process is shown above. First, bacteria accumulate on the side of the tooth. If not removed in 24 hours, the bacteria harden and work their way down, forming a pocket beneath the gum which is inaccessible to the toothbrush. The bacteria then begin to attack the surrounding bone. If not checked in time, the tooth will become loose in the mouth.

substances in food and saliva. This contains up to 300 different organisms, some of which are toxic, capable of eating into the gum tissue and initiating the slow, insidious process of gum disease. If you have managed to keep all your teeth by the age of 16, the chances are that any subsequent loss will be caused, not by decay, but by infected gums. As plaque becomes damaging within 24 hours of formation, the teeth must be thoroughly brushed at least once, preferably twice, a day.

Protecting your gums

Gum disease is almost universal. Tell-tale signs are puffy, inflamed gums, which bleed on brushing, and soreness. Although the process can be halted and, to some extent, reversed, as long as the tooth is still in the mouth and has some bone around it, the measures necessary become increasingly radical, time-consuming and expensive as the disease progresses. In its early stages, however, you can brush and floss your way out of it.

Vigilance is all-important — both on the part of your dentist, who should make a gum inspection an integral part of every visit, and on your own part, as professional attention will do little to safeguard the health of your gums if you do not look after them conscientiously in the meantime.

Seeing your dentist

Do not wait until you find a hole in your tooth or are struck down with toothache before seeing your dentist. You should have regular check-ups at six-monthly intervals, unless your dentist specifies otherwise. These check-ups will enable your dentist to establish that there is no decay, that your gums are sound and healthy and that there is no untoward change in the mouth, such as the eruption of wisdom teeth, that might alter the position of your teeth and affect your bite.

You should also make a point of seeing a dental hygienist at least once a year, so that you can have any tartar, a hard calcium deposit in the plaque, removed and your mouth professionally cleaned. Many dental practices now have a hygienist. If yours does not, ask your dentist to refer you to one. A really good teaching programme on cleaning and caring for your teeth will stand you in good stead.

To test a toothbrush: run the bristles backwards and forwards over the back of your hand. They should feel comfortable, even soothing – not scratchy – and should flow evenly over the contours of your knuckles. If they don't, don't use it.

	Description	Comments
Crowns	An artificial 'cap' is cemented on to a tooth, already fined down to about half of its original diameter, so that the crown slips easily over the top. Material used depends on the position of the tooth in the mouth. Porcelain is the most natural looking but does not have the strength to withstand constant pressure, and is therefore used only on the front teeth. Gold is often used at the back, where strength counts most and appearance matters least.	Unless badly fitted and barring unforeseen accidents, crowns are permanent and tend to 'age' well, staining and discolouring at much the same rate as natural teeth. The cement fills a space between the crown and the tooth and, if infection is allowed to creep in, decay can occur behind the crown. This can result in loss of bone, infected nerves, abscesses or gum disease.
Bridges	These are used to attach one or more 'dummy' teeth to the surrounding teeth, using crowns on either side to anchor the new tooth into position. Bridges are usually made from gold or a gold and metal alloy and covered with porcelain.	An excellent solution for a missing front tooth, as the new dummy tooth stays firmly in place and cuts out the need for dentures. Badly done, the bridge may be ill-fitting and the dummy tooth may look unnatural and false.
Veneers	Veneers are pre-moulded covers, rather like artificial fingernails in appearance. They are bonded on to the tooth with a special adhesive, or are painted on to the tooth in layers and left to 'set' in the mouth.	Veneers are cheap, require very little preparation and are easy to fit. They can be used to disguise a badly stained tooth but are most useful on children who have a chipped/broken front tooth. Unfortunately, they tend to stain and discolour easily.
Implants	Implants are metal stumps which are fixed into the jaw bone and then crowned. The idea, though not often the reality, is that, if large gaps between the teeth can be 'crowned' in this way, there will be no need for false teeth.	There are very few advantages. For some, but by no means all, people who are able to tolerate them, implants may be preferable to false teeth, in a cosmetic sense. They are rarely preferable in a medical sense, however, because of rejection and infection.

Cosmetic dentistry is a misleading term. While crowns, bridges and veneers can do much to improve the appearance of the teeth, nothing is more attractive than an uncluttered mouth, with no tell-tale flashes of gold, nickel or even porcelain. On the whole, the less you do to a tooth, with the exception of orthodontics and the removal of decay, the better and stronger it will be.

Cosmetic dentistry is always expensive, but the results can be extremely good and many consider that these justify the expense. While it is essential that any dentistry is carried out by a good and competent dentist, it is especially important in the cosmetic field where mistakes are invariably expensive and often extremely difficult to put right.

nails

Nails, rewardingly, will repay every minute spent looking after them — provided that you manicure them properly and protect your hands from damaging influences. Look at them carefully, then answer the following

1. Are your nails the same colour as the skin beneath them (or the palm of your hand if you are dark skinned)?
a) yes **b)** no, they are significantly lighter or darker

2. Is the nail surface
a) smooth and even **b)** ridged?

3. Are your nails brittle and inclined to break easily?
a) no **b)** yes

4. Do you wear rubber gloves for wet domestic chores?
a) yes **b)** no

5. Do you do a lot of housework, gardening and/or decorating?
a) no **b)** yes

6. Are your cuticles damaged – cut, puffy or sore?
a) no **b)** yes

7. Do you ever use anything made from steel, including scissors, when manicuring your nails?
a) no **b)** yes

8. When you manicure your nails, do you cut or trim the cuticle?
a) no **b)** yes

Questions 1-3 are designed to give you an insight into your general health, as it is reflected in the condition of your nails. **b** answers indicate that it is not – or recently has not been – as good as it might.

Questions 4-8 are designed to check on how carefully you look after your nails. If you answered **b** to any of these, your less-than-perfect nails are probably owing to careless manicuring or to exposure to damaging chemicals, such as detergents and nail varnish remover.

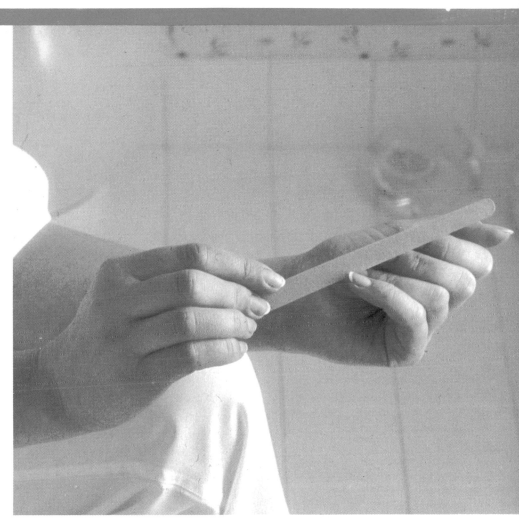

Nails start growing from matrix cells situated about 3-4 mm from the base of the nail. By the time they become visible they are often completely dead, though a patch of live nail can sometimes be seen at the white half moon. Any damage here may cause the nail to grow out unevenly.

File rather than cut as cutting can weaken the nail and cause it to flake. File in one direction only, from sides to centre, using the softer (lighter) side of an emery board, <u>not</u> a metal file. Aim for a rounded tip: the shape at the tip should reflect the shape at the base to make a perfect oval, as left.

Manicure step by step

Over-enthusiastic manicuring can injure the nail and damage the cuticle, particularly if sharp-ended, metal instruments are used. Signs of bad manicuring are ridges, dents or nicks along the nails and a pink inflamed cuticle. Consistent use of heavy lacquers, together with the chemical solvents needed to remove them, particularly acetone, will dry out the nail. So while your first impulse might be to disguise out-of-condition nails with a coating of colour, you would be wiser to leave them to themselves, giving regular manicures. Soak the fingertips in a bowl of warm olive oil for a few minutes each week and see the difference. If your nails are in good condition and you want to use nail colour, use it with restraint and try to give your nails an occasional rest. Fragile nails may benefit from a technique known as 'wrapping', which bolsters the strength of the nail. It must be carried out by a competent manicurist.

Start by soaking the fingers briefly in a bowl of warm water to which you have added a slice of lemon, to loosen dirt beneath the tips. (If nails are very dry, soak them in warmed olive or almond oil instead.) Dry and scrape away any loosened dirt with an orange stick. Do not poke or prod. If dirt has become embedded in the pink part of the nail, let it grow out.

Massage cuticle cream well into the cuticle and surrounding nail using the ball of the thumb in a firm rotating movement.

File down the sharp end of an orange stick so that it is smooth and gently slide it a little way under the cuticle at the base and sides of the nail, lifting the cuticle slightly. Be gentle: never use an orange stick with a pointed or metal end; never clip the cuticle and avoid cuticle 'removers'.

Rub a generous amount of hand cream on to the hand, and massage in as though putting on a pair of gloves. See next page if applying varnish.

nailsnailsnails

When applying varnish, first ensure that any traces of the old colour are removed. Remove varnish around the cuticle by wrapping cotton wool around an orange stick and dipping it in the remover. Begin with a clear base coat to prevent pigments being absorbed, follow with two coats of colour (three if frosted). Allow each coat to dry. Finish with a top coat of clear polish to seal in colour and add gloss.

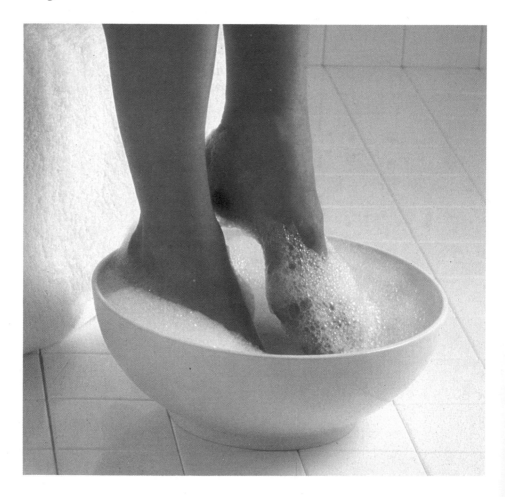

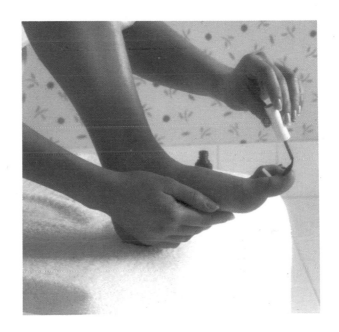

Pedicure step by step

Start by soaking the feet in a warm footbath. Temperature should be about 40°C (104°F). To make a traditional footbath: add a teacupful of Epsom salts or ordinary sea salt to every 4½ litres/ 1 gallon (10 US pints) hot water.

Once the feet are soaked, and the skin soft, take a pumice stone, rough skin remover or chiropody sponge and remove any hard dead skin. Dry your feet and inspect them. Take any obvious or incipient problems to a registered chiropodist. Cut nails square along the top, following the shape of the toe and taking care not to cut them too short. Smooth sharp corners with the coarse (darker) side of an emery board.

Repeat the cuticle cream/orange stick routine, described on previous page, and then apply cream, rubbing in well and avoiding the spaces between the toes.

cosmetics

1. Is your natural colouring
a) very pale, with no pink or orange in the skin **b)** fair with a pinkish colour **c)** reddish **d)** sallow **e)** olive **f)** brown or black?

2. Is your foundation
a) the same colour as your skin **b)** lighter **c)** darker

3. Where do you test for colour when buying foundation?
a) on the back of your hand **b)** on your face

4. Is the predominant colour tone in your foundation
a) ivory **b)** light with a hint of pink **c)** light to mid-beige **d)** cream with a tinge of bronze **e)** mid-beige **f)** tan brown or dark brown?

5. Which best describes your blusher colour?
a) light shimmery pink or mid-pink **b)** bright pink, peach or coral **c)** tawny brown or chestnut **d)** bronze **e)** tawny red **f)** strong deep pink, such as fuchsia or raspberry

6. Are your lip colour and blusher
a) the same general colour family **b)** completely different in colour?

7. Are your eyes
a) blue or grey **b)** green or hazel **c)** brown?

8. Which of these eye colours/colour combinations do you like?
a) silver/lilac shading with grey to emphasize **b)** pink/gold shading with brown to emphasize **c)** soft beige/pink/apricot shading with charcoal to emphasize **d)** soft neutral colours – pinks, beiges, browns **e)** pastel colours – powder blue or pink and green **f)** strong, solid colours – bright blue, deep pinks and purples?

Here, as in real life, blusher and foundation tones should match up with natural colouring. Hence, if you answered **a** for question 1, you should have also answered **a** for questions 4 and 5. Foundation should always match skin (2) – the skin of your face, not your hand (3). If the skin is naturally dark (**1d**, perhaps, **1e**, and **1f**), the foundation can be a tone or two darker, but going lighter makes any face masklike. Lip colours and blushers should also coordinate (6). Almost any colour can look good on almost any colour eye. Particularly effective combinations: **8a** for **7a**; **8b** for **7b**; **8c** for **7c**. **8d** is good for anyone and a marvellous, natural daytime look.

There are no absolute rules about make-up colours. Unusual combinations of colour, even obvious contradictions, can be very effective – but you must know what you are doing. This quiz aims to guide, not to dictate. If you already have a colour scheme that works well for you, fine. If not, complete the questionnaire to see where you might be going wrong and to get some fresh ideas.

44

Used sensibly and with reasonable regularity, most cosmetics will last just as long as you want them to. If used carelessly or applied only infrequently, you run the risk of irritation and/or infection from bacteria which will eventually form in even the most stable of products. Homemade cosmetics have about the same shelf-life as foods, must always be kept in the refrigerator and should not be used after a week. The shelf-life of commercial products is much longer. Products most susceptible to contamination by air, house dust or dirty fingers are those using cream formulae, such as moisturizers, eye colours and lipsticks. Powder- and alcohol-based cosmetics, on the other hand, will last longer. But remember to balance medical and aesthetic considerations. When your product starts to separate or discolour, lose its fragrance, flake, cake or harden, replace it.

● Heat, light, air and moisture all have a damaging effect on cosmetics and perfumes. Keep them in a cool, dark place and ensure all containers are air- and water-tight.

● All cosmetics are subject to contamination from oxygen in the air — cosmetics in open-top jars much more so than those in tubes. Always replace tops after use.

● Keep your cosmetics to yourself. One study of over 1,000 eye cosmetics showed that, although they were free from germs on purchase, nearly half had developed some degree of bacterial activity after six months. Most had been used on more than one set of eyes.

● Clean fingers are the safest cosmetic applicators of all, particularly if using cream-based cosmetic products, as bacteria and germs can cling to the greasy residue left on sponges and brushes. Replace brushes every year and cream eye shadow applicators and sponges every six months. Be particularly careful with mascara applicators, because these pick up germs very readily.

When you consider that there are over 100,000 differently formulated cosmetics, using several thousand ingredients, it is surprising not that some people develop allergies or sensitivities to one or more of them, but that so few of us do. The processes by which cosmetics are made are so carefully controlled and the ingredients so scrupulously screened, that most of us can put anything we choose on to our skins with absolute confidence and in perfect safety. Even so, there is always a chance of reacting adversely to a product at some time in our lives and it may quite possibly be one which we have been using happily for months or even years. Caution is the watchword.

carecarecare

'There is no excellent beauty which hath not some strangeness in the proportion' said Sir Francis Bacon 300 years ago, recognizing that interest and beauty in a face derive much more from how the features work together than on how symmetrically 'perfect' they are.

Beginning your self-analysis with a similar appreciation of harmony, make the most of your face by working with it — accentuate the good, minimize the not-so-good and rebalance the shape where necessary. Make-up can help you to do this, but first consider your features not in isolation but in relation to each other — length of face in terms of width, shape of nose in terms of shape of chin, line of eyebrow in terms of line of eye. Measure your face to see how it compares with the 'perfect' proportions given below. This will help you towards a better appreciation both of its general shape and of the relation of your features to each other — how close together your eyes are set, for example...

Feature	Measurement/comments	'Perfect'
Length of face		1 ½ x width
Width of face		⅔ of length
Width of jaw		slightly less than face
Eye spacing		1 eye length

Take off your make-up and pull your hair well away from your face. Taking a ruler and holding it absolutely straight, measure length of face from top of forehead to tip of chin (bottom right). Be as precise as possible and measure in centimetres, not in inches. Continue by measuring the widest part of face (usually along top of cheekbone, as top right). The

measuringmeasuring

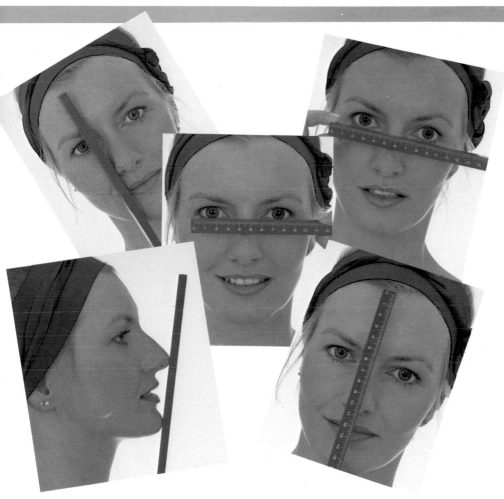

perfect oval-shaped face has a length that is one and a half times width. If width is two-thirds or more of length, the face is wide (usually round). If length is more than one and three-quarters of width, the face is long. Now measure your face across the jawbone. If it is significantly less than width measurement and chin is pointed, the face is heart shaped.

If it is the same and chin is blunt, the face is probably square. Assess width of mouth by placing ruler at the outside corner of mouth so that it lies parallel with bridge of nose (above left). Look straight ahead. The outside edge of ruler should line up with inner edge of iris.
Test your profile by placing ruler against your nose and

chin (below left). Your lips should come well within it. If they touch ruler, chin is weak. Measure the distance between your eyes (centre). It should come one eye's length. If less than three-quarters of length, the eyes are close set; if more than one and a quarter times length, they are wide spaced.

A flattering hairstyle creates the right frame for the face. When did you last think of changing yours?

Eyebrows should be natural but not unruly. If they are too sparse, allow them to grow out. If too luxuriant, thin them.

Are your eyes round or oval or almond-shaped, large or small? Make more of their shape and size with careful shading.

Dark circles detract from eyes that would otherwise enchant. Camouflage with a light concealer stick.

High cheekbones are an inherited blessing. If you have to suck in your cheeks to see them, take heart: careful use of light and shadow can 'lift' them.

Noses that are broad at the bridge or the base can be narrowed by using a darker toned foundation. Noses that are crooked can be 'straightened'.

Skin should be smooth and even in tone and texture. While the right type and shade of foundation will help to refine a complexion, problem skins need skincare first, make-up second.

Lip pencils, a firm hand and the use of two shades of lipstick will help rebalance your mouth.

A heavy jawline? The use of a darker foundation blended up over the weighty part will lighten it.

detailsdetails

The smoothest way to apply foundation: dot it on forehead, nose, cheeks and chin, keeping to the centre of face and away from hairline. Then, using a slightly damp sponge, or fingers, blend outwards. Smooth some gently on and around the eyelids and lips too. Take foundation as far down the neck as will be showing. Finally, check that foundation is evenly blended around jaw, just under nose, and around the hairline.

Conceal dark circles under eyes and any other darker patches on face with a concealer stick just a shade or two lighter than your natural skintone. Press in with clean fingers over the foundation.

To take the colour out of a pimple, use a small make-up brush, dab it on to a concealer that is the same shade as your natural skin tone and stroke the spot gently. This will help to cover all the contours of the spot.

basebasebase

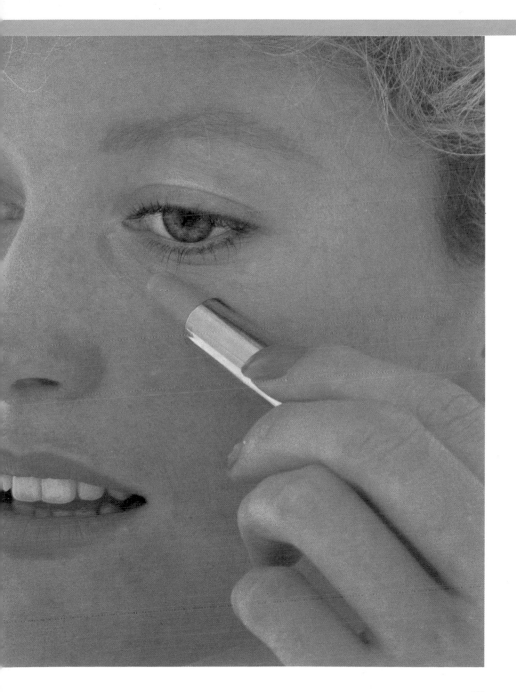

Begin your make-up with a good, even base. If you are fortunate enough to possess one naturally, a plain or tinted gel moisturizer with a light dusting of blusher over the cheekbones is probably the best daytime look. If the skin is blotchy in colour, or uneven in texture, a foundation will help to even out skin colour, making the complexion appear smooth and refined.

If the skin is dry, moisturize first, allow your skin five or 10 minutes to 'settle' and then use a hydrating foundation. There should be no sign of greasiness, certainly no shine, when you start. If the skin is oily, use a good astringent first to remove any immediate oil on the skin and cover with a medicated or matt foundation. Transparent gels and tinted moisturizers can look marvellous on a good, healthy skin.

Aim for a foundation that is as close as possible to your natural skin tone. Try to avoid shades that have a lot of pink in them (not good for any colour type) and go instead for a colour base that complements your natural colouring. Always test a foundation on your face, not on the back of your hand. You only have to put your hand up to your face to see the difference in colour between them. Be sure to continue the colour as far down your neck as will be showing.

Once you have applied the foundation, conceal or contour where necessary (see right). For the purposes of shading or contouring you will need a foundation two

Narrow a nose that is too broad at the bridge or base by drawing triangles of foundation about three shades deeper than your skin tone on either side of the wide area (1). Then blend into make-up. Intensify the effect by adding blusher.

For an even foundation blend outwards, following arrows.

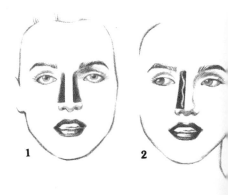

1

2

shades or so darker than your natural skin tone and — most important — a light hand. Blushers and shaders that are incompletely blended can make the face look bruised or striped.

Special covering creams camouflage surface scars admirably — and they are equally effective for birth marks, broken veins and dark circles around the eyes. These dark circles are caused not so much by late nights and lack of sleep as by a natural thinness of the skin, making blood vessels more visible because they are closer to the surface. In addition, the brow and cheekbones cast their own shadows. While concealing creams can be useful for taking the colour out of a pimple, they will not conceal it entirely. A bump in the skin will always show in certain lights. As the head is always turning and the face moving, the light is bound to strike it unflatteringly from time to time. It is therefore worth giving more thought to prevention than to concealment. Spots will disappear more rapidly if not smothered with make-up.

shadeshade

Straighten a nose that is slightly crooked by applying a darker toned foundation along the crooked side (2), a lighter one on the other.

Lift a heavy jaw by applying a darker foundation in a long triangle just above the weighty part (3) and blending it into the lighter more natural shade on the face and neck.

Lift cheekbones with clever use of shadow and light. But do not forget to blend. The effect should be that of a shadow cast quite naturally by the bone, not a diagonal stripe. Suck in your cheeks to find your cheekbones. Place a triangle of the darker foundation colour in this hollow – the widest part extending towards the ears (4). Blend and add highlight across the bone above (5).

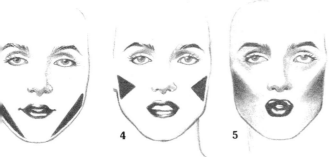

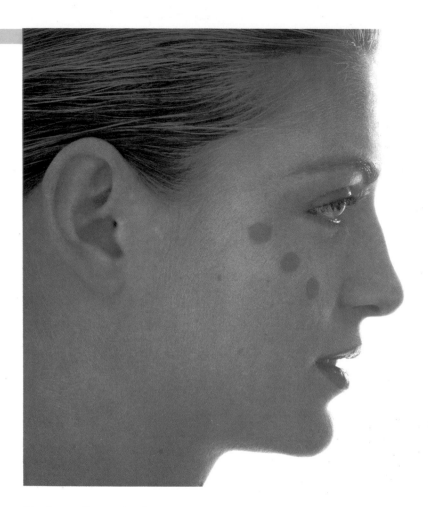

Blusher enlivens the face, adds colour and polish and, when whisked over eyelid and browbone, gives a natural no-make-up look for daytime. The art in using it lies in three things. The first is picking the right colour (see colour quiz, page 44). The second is knowing where to apply it (see right) and the third is knowing how much to use. Start with the lightest touch and build up from there.

Of the three basic blushers, gels are best applied over a moisturizer, or a light foundation, with no powder; cream blushers on top of foundation but under powder; powder blushers over powder...

Unless aiming for a dramatic effect, blushers and lip colours should complement each other. In fact, you can improvise by using your lip colour on your cheeks in place of blusher. As a rule: the lighter the skin tone, the lighter the blusher. Apply blusher along the cheekbones (above). Add Iridescent highlights above for shine; darker shading beneath for more emphasis.

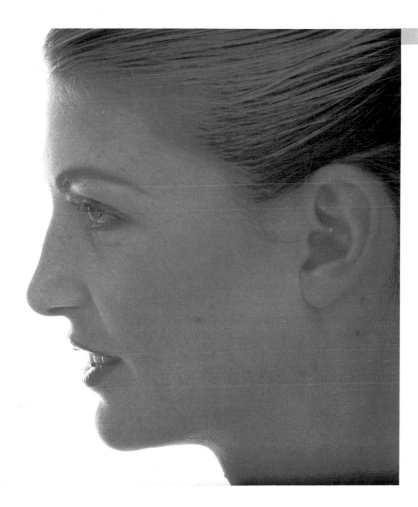

To find your starting point:
look straight at yourself in a
mirror and place blusher
directly below each eyeball.

For evenings and an exotic
look, apply iridescent
blusher to temples, earlobes,
chin and across the nose . . .

blushblushblush

Loose face powder is the best
way to set a make-up.
Choose a fine translucent
powder and apply it liberally
on a young face, sparingly on
an older one.

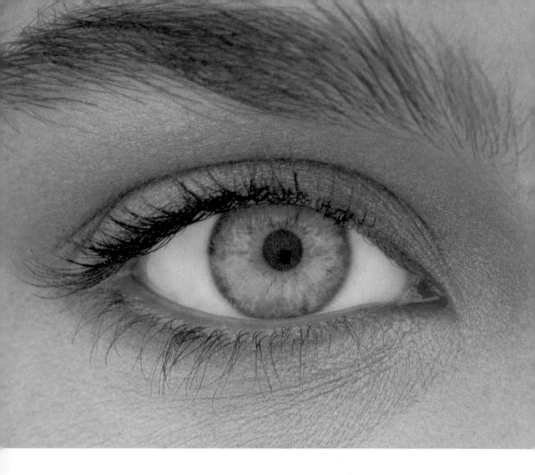

eyeseyeseyes

Widen eyes set too close together: shade a dark triangle across the outer corners of the upper eyelid.

Minimize the space between the eyes if they are wide-set, by blending shadow across the inner halves of upper lid and up towards the browbone. Slant shadow on outer corners of lower lid.

Before making up eyes, check foundation is smooth, dark rings camouflaged and all powder settled. Thin eyebrows, if necessary, and brush upwards for an instant wide-awake look. If brows are too sparse, fill in with light feathery strokes using an appropriately coloured eyebrow pencil. Take a soft eye pencil and line lids top and bottom, preferably outside the lashes, keeping pencil at a flattish angle to the eye and hand steady. Neutral colours, such as charcoal, brown and grey, are the most natural while the more vibrant colours can look sensational at night. Remember to stop your line just short of the inner corners of the eye to avoid a narrowing effect and then use the same pencil to emphasize the natural contour at the crease. Choose a shadow that tones well with your eye pencil and smudge it over the upper lids, blending it down into the line and up into the crease. Continue building colour to intensify the effect. Add highlight to browbone, using clean fingers or applicator, for a more elaborate make-up. Finish with several thin coats of mascara, letting lashes dry and separating them between each coat.

Lift droopy eyes by drawing a thin line at the inner corner of upper lid and steadily widening it so that it covers the outer corner of the lid entirely.

Make small eyes appear larger. Line inside of lids with soft white pencil. Use a smoky grey or brown pencil underneath lower lashes. Finish with black mascara.

Elongate round eyes by lining insides of upper lids, outer half of lower ones. Apply shadow at corner, as shown.

Bring deep-set eyes forward, by lining outer halves of lids with darkish pencil, widening line as you go. Then apply a lighter shadow and smudge out.

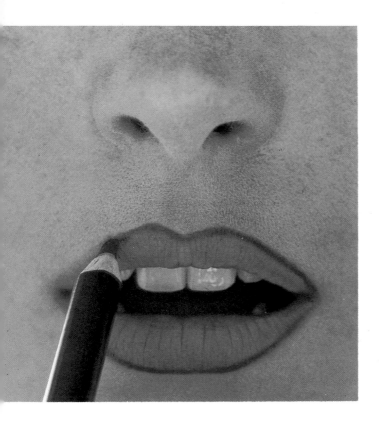

Lipcolour will add the finishing touch to your make-up. Prime first with a good base: smooth foundation onto lips (medicated ones are particularly good as they dry lips out and help colour to last), and follow with a dusting of powder. If lipcolour tends to 'bleed' into the fine lines above the mouth, apply your colour twice — once before and once after the powder. Next outline lips with a soft lip pencil just a tone or two darker than your chosen colour and blot with a tissue to soften the line. Then fill in with your chosen lip shade, using an applicator or, preferably, a thin lip brush. Finish with a transparent gloss. If a natural look is required, use a clear or tinted gloss in place of colour.

To line lips, place fore and middle fingers at each corner of the mouth so that the lips are taut. You will find it much easier to draw a steady line.

lipslipslipslips

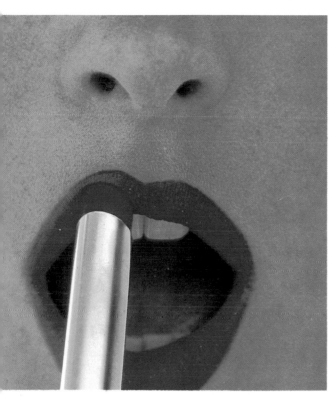

To make your upper or lower lip less full, line just inside your natural lipline with a colour as close to your own natural skin colour as possible. Then fill in.

To make the whole mouth less prominent, use two lipstick shades. Fill in the centre section of both lips with the darker tone of your chosen lip colour. Apply the lighter one to either side and blend inwards with a clean lipbrush.

To add fullness to the upper or lower lip, take a white pencil and draw a line just outside your natural lipline. Go over the line with lipstick and fill in.

amam

<u>For daytime,</u> concentrate on smoothing out skintone, adding a touch of colour to face and definition to eyes and mouth. Here, a light moisturizing foundation is applied to the skin and dark circles around the eyes are concealed. A soft pink blusher is brushed over the cheekbones, across browbone and lightly whisked around temples and hairline for a healthy glow. Eyes are defined with a neutral brown below and soft cinnamon above. A light natural pink lipcolour adds the finishing touch, with just a slick of transparent gloss.

pmpm

<u>For evening,</u> build on blusher, eye and lip colours to intensify the effect. Use more blusher, or a more vibrant tone, over cheekbones and dab it lightly on tip of nose and chin for a warm 'party' look. A light dusting of pearly translucent powder will add shine. Here, a dark bronze is used to define the eyes and then continued out to the corners to emphasize their natural shape. The lids are lined with black and the browbone highlit with gleaming gold. Lips are outlined with lip pencil, then painted deep red.

<u>Make-up.</u> Correct uneven skin tones with a tinted mois-
turizer or carefully matched shade of foundation. If necessary, blend your own colour from two or more different
shades until you get it right. Use blusher to give a polished
sheen to the face and highlight to intensify the effect. Or
use highlight only: a transparent white or pink over
cheekbones and temples. Strong vibrant colours on
cheeks, lips and eyes can also be used to dramatic effect
(see suggestions above right).

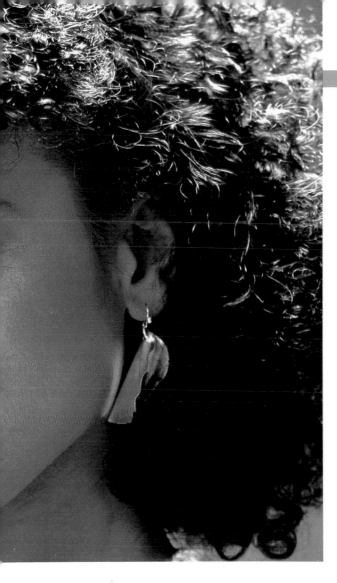

Here, skin is evened out with the model's own foundation which she blends herself, and a soft coral cream blusher smoothed over cheekbones. Eyelids are lined in black and shaded brown, blended into pink across the brow and defined with lots of black mascara. Lips are painted a reddish coral.

Alternative colour suggestions: try strong peacock colours (bright pinks and blues) on eyes, deep fuschia or raspberry pink on cheeks and lips. Burgundies and purple shades are also good for the eyes, as is gold for a more exotic look . . .

blackblack

Hair. Black hair is often coarse and usually dry but it can look marvellous when well conditioned. Try a weekly oil treatment using a pleasantly scented vegetable oil, such as almond, apricot or peach kernel. Leave on for 30 minutes and remove by adding shampoo first, then rinsing with water. Avoid straightening hair. Sew artificial braids on to the hair, or use brightly coloured combs instead. For more shine and a larger, looser curl, use a setting lotion after shampooing and finger dry to shape.

Here, skin tone is smoothed with its matching foundation and the lightest dusting of powder on the centre of the face. The soft peach tones of the shirt are reflected in the soft peach cheek colour and slightly richer lip shade. Eyes are shaded to their natural colour – grey/green – and emphasized with mascara, brown not black.

Alternative make-up: define eyes in soft brown or grey and add colour to enliven face. Try pinks and lilacs or mauves across the eyes, with peaches, corals and soft pinks on cheeks and lips.

greygrey

Beauty points for 40 plus

Health is your first priority if you want to preserve your looks from the advancing years. Start with regular exercise, concentrating particularly on the loosening sequences (blue leotard) in the Shape chapter, plenty of fresh air and sleep, a balanced diet and regular health checks.

Skincare and make-up techniques should be rethought every five years from the age of about 40. Skin that has become drier and looks flaky in patches needs a mild exfoliant once a week and a rich moisturizer at night. The throat and neck tend to age particularly rapidly, so always start moisturizing from the collar bone up. Increased facial hair caused by declining levels of oestrogen, can be a problem after the menopause. Treat it temporarily by bleaching or permanently by electrolysis.

Cosmetics can subtract years from the look of the face but unless you are very careful they may add them instead. Layers of foundation and face powder can be very ageing because they tend to settle into creases in the skin, bringing out every line. Use a light hand: apply a thin layer of moisturizing foundation with a slightly damp sponge and cover with a translucent dusting of powder, keeping to the barest minimum around the eyes where wrinkles are all too easily emphasized.

Complexion tones change as you grow older so make sure foundation, blusher, eye and lip shades are still appropriate. Choose a foundation as close to your natural colour as possible and keep blusher, lip, nail and eye colours soft and positive to counteract greyness. Outlaw black mascara, eyeliner and frosted colour shadows.

Hair fades with skin. Respect this mutual mellowing: striving to recapture your old colour when you start to go grey can produce an unhappy, jarring contrast between skin and hair tones. Have the lightest strands brightened a shade or two, instead, for a head of soft, natural highlights. If your own natural colour is very dark, lighten the base a little for a softer, more subtle effect.

All scents are built 'note' by 'note', according to an evaporation scale, so that together they will create an amalgamated 'chord'.

The top note is the most volatile part of the fragrance. It has the most immediate effect on the sense of smell, evaporates into the air in seconds, gives the first fleeting impression and remains for about 10 to 20 minutes, before gradually subsiding as the lower notes develop. Examples: bergamot, lemon, lavender, mint, *bois de rose*, coriander.

The middle note is the 'heart' of the perfume and carries the scent for about 20 to 30 minutes, while the base note is developing. It usually takes 10 to 20 minutes to develop and lasts for two to three hours. Examples: *Rose de Bulgarie*, jasmine, neroli, galbanum, verbena, lily-of-the-valley, ylang-ylang.

The base note determines the holding power of a fragrance and is the true characteristic from which the rest of the smell will be created. Initially strong and unpleasant smelling, base notes can take up to half an hour to develop their 'true' smell, when they will be quite beautiful. The base note lingers for six hours or more and, once all evaporation has taken place, a small residual part of it will remain for months or even years. This is known as the dry-out. Examples: patchouli, vetivert, oakmoss, orris, jasmine, sandalwood, cedarwood, artificial musks.

SCENT

There are no hard and fast rules about wearing scent. Every scent you buy becomes emphatically your own from the moment you spray it on. Your body chemistry is the main determinant of whether a fragrance will work well for you. Once you have found one that does, bear the following in mind.

Apply it to the pulse points — those places where the blood vessels are nearer the surface of the skin and body temperature is slightly warmer (hairline, nape of neck, behind ears, under breasts, in crook of arm, inside wrists and knees and on either side of ankles). Warmth encourages evaporation and allows the bouquet to develop.

Spray a fragrance onto hair or the lining of clothes but not directly onto fabrics as the residual oil will stain.

Repeat applications about every four hours to give a fresh burst of the fragrance. Look after scents well to preserve them for as long as possible. Store them in a cool, dark, dry place and replace stoppers firmly after use.

TYPE	COMPRISES	LASTS
EXTRAIT or **PARFUM**	15-20 per cent perfume; 80-85 per cent spirit.	Two to six hours, depending on your body chemistry. The *extrait* is the truest expression of the perfume. Sometimes, part of the spirit (alcohol) content is replaced by an oil. This increases the 'staying power' by slowing down the rate of evaporation.
PARFUM DE TOILETTE	12-15 per cent perfume; mostly spirit; some water.	Two to five hours. This was developed in the USA to provide a stronger and longer lasting alternative to the *eau de toilette*.
EAU DE TOILETTE	5-12 per cent perfume; more water than spirit.	Two to four hours. The higher water content makes for a greater degree of dilution and so faster evaporation. Dab or spray on lavishly
EAU DE COLOGNE	2-6 per cent perfume; predominantly water; some spirit.	One to two hours. *Eaux de Cologne*, which developed out of the original *Kölnischwasser*, are created to give only the lightest veil of fragrance. They are refreshing, delicate and marvellously revitalizing.

shape

Being in good shape is where health and beauty meet: you look good, feel alert, alive and ready for anything.

Although shape can be improved, often dramatically, by better posture, firming exercises and shedding excess weight, there are certain elements you cannot change. So be realistic. Recognize you have a basic body type (see page 74) and work with what you have.

What would you like to change? Appraise your shape honestly, considering good points as well as bad. Work out your aims and then give yourself three months in which to get into really good physical shape...

Less-than-perfect aspects of your shape are much more likely to be owing to a less-than-perfect lifestyle than to anything intrinsically wrong with your body...

How do you measure up?

Measuring can be just as useful a gauge to progress as weighing yourself. The key is to look at your body as an integrated whole. Consider measurements in relation to each other and not just independently.

Measure yourself at bust when breathing in, at narrowest part of waist and at widest part of hips, thighs and calves. Note them down, below, and then subtract each from your hip measurement. Ideally, bust and hips should be the same and waist, thighs and calves about 25, 41 and 56 cm (10, 16 and 22 inches) less than this respectively. These are the dimensions to work towards, but remember they are approximations only — not an absolute set of statistics.

	Bust	Waist	Hips	Thighs	Calves
now					
+ 3 months					

The critical changeable elements in any shape strategy are posture, exercise and diet. The constant is your body type. Identifying and accepting your body type — learning to like yourself the way you fundamentally are — is where body wisdom starts. This is healthy realism not complacency. Excess weight and out-of-condition muscles do not belong to any of the three basic types shown below. So distinguish between the imperfections you can do something about and the inherited characteristics you cannot, *then* take yourself to task...

The ectomorph is lean and angular with long limbs, narrow joints, low body fat and muscle and few curves.

The mesomorph is reasonably compact, with broad shoulders and pelvic girdle and well-developed muscles, particularly at calf and forearm.

The endomorph is shorter limbed, has a lower centre of gravity, wider hips, a higher proportion of fat to muscle and a tendency to put on weight easily.

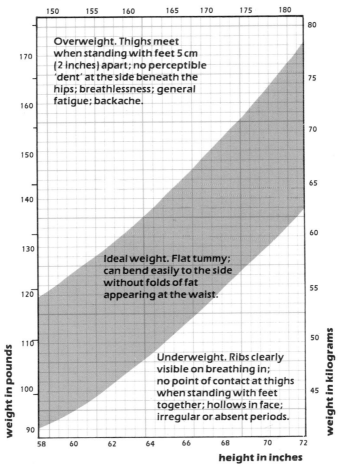

height in centimetres

Overweight. Thighs meet when standing with feet 5 cm (2 inches) apart; no perceptible 'dent' at the side beneath the hips; breathlessness; general fatigue; backache.

Ideal weight. Flat tummy; can bend easily to the side without folds of fat appearing at the waist.

Underweight. Ribs clearly visible on breathing in; no point of contact at thighs when standing with feet together; hollows in face; irregular or absent periods.

weight in pounds

weight in kilograms

height in inches

The weight graph, above, is based on national insurance figures and shows very broadly the weight range appropriate for your height.

Check you come within it. Then look at the notes on under, over and ideal weight. These should help you to be more precise.

Best time to weigh yourself: in the morning, before dressing and breakfast, and after going to the lavatory.

How are you sitting as you read this? Are your shoulders in line with each other, your back straight, your weight evenly distributed on both buttocks, your knees relaxed and parallel? Or are you slumping forwards, with your neck curved and your spine rounded, one shoulder higher than the other, your legs crossed and your weight supported on your elbows? If so, you may be in perfect physical shape but you certainly will not look it.

Of all the shape determinants, the most immediate is posture. Diet and exercise may give you the figure you want but if you do not hold it correctly, it will never be seen to advantage...

How symmetrical are you? Look at...
Front and back: is head centrally balanced? Are shoulders, hips (buttocks), fingertips and knees all level? Is your weight evenly distributed on both feet?
Profile: would a straight line pass behind your shoulder, down through your knee and out just in front of your ankle, as shown below? If not, try to identify what is causing your body to be out of line...

Daily posture improvers.
Counteract the forward pull
of gravity and a sedentary
lifestyle with shoulder
rotations. Stand as shown,
right, arms outstretched at
shoulder level, hands
making loose fists. Rotate
shoulders back and down,
away from the ears. Be
careful not to let arms and
hands drop too.

Centering the pelvis will
encourage exaggerated
arches in the spine to
lengthen out. Start by
standing against a wall. If
you can get your hand
between the small of your
back and the wall, your spine
is too arched, as right. Bend
your knees and then tilt your
pelvis upwards, far right.
Hold, release. Repeat several
times. Then gradually
straighten up the wall again.
Notice how much flatter your
back is.

We get so used to standing incorrectly that it is difficult to
assess posture faults simply by looking in a mirror. Ask a
friend to take three full-length photographs of you, back,
front and profile, as left. Wear a leotard so that you will be
able to see the line of your body quite clearly. Make sure
the edge of the viewfinder is lined up with a vertical plane
such as the edge of a door. Once the photographs are
developed, take a pen and a ruler. Lining the ruler up
against the parallel edge of the photograph — not
against the line of your body — draw a series of lines, as
shown left. You now have a set of geometrical reference
points to show you how symmetrical you are.

**A finely tuned sense of
balance is essential for
posture. Test yours by taking
up the 'tree' position, above:
one foot on the floor, the
other resting as far up the
inner thigh as possible...
You should feel quite
comfortable in this pose.**

77

To test for suppleness at shoulders... Stand or kneel, place your left arm along your back and take your right arm over your shoulder to meet it. If you can clasp your fingers together you have good rotation at the shoulder joint; If your fingers meet, fair; if they fail to touch, poor. (Try both sides; one shoulder is often stiffer than the other.)

...and spine. Kneel down on all fours. Keeping hands in line with shoulders, drop your forehead down and bring your knee up to meet it, as shown. If you can touch your head with your knee without straining, you have good spinal mobility; if they almost meet, fair; if they are some way apart, poor.

testingtesting

Test suppleness and strength. Suppleness is determined by the ease with which you can move your joints through their full range — bending, twisting and turning freely and gracefully. Try these two exercises to see how well you do. Strength is also important for ease of movement and helps define the line of the body. Strong, conditioned muscles give a sleek contour and so improve appearance. Do you need to work at toning and firming yours?

To test for strength in legs...
Start by standing with your
back to the wall. Now
gradually bend your knees
and bring your feet away
from the wall until you are
'sitting' with your thighs
parallel to the floor. How
long can you stay there?
Over 90 seconds (60 if over
50) good; 60 to 90 seconds
(40 and 60 if over 50) fair; less
than 60 seconds (40 if over
50) poor.

... and in chest, arms and
shoulders. Place a table
against a wall so that it is
quite steady. Now, do a
series of modified press-ups,
with hands shoulder-width
apart and back as straight as
possible, trying not to arch
or to hollow your spine.
Bend both arms and bring
your chest to the table, then
straighten them. Do as many
as you can without straining
and then stop. How many
did you do? More than 15 (10
if over 50) good; between 10
and 15 (seven and 10 if over
50) fair; less than 10 (seven if
over 50) poor. A poor score
indicates that you should
work at increasing the
strength of chest, arm and
shoulder muscles.

daily exercise programme

These exercises are divided into two sections: a daily programme which combines loosening exercises (blue leotard) with firming ones (red leotard) and a sequence at the end designed to give a really good general workout (yellow leotard).

The secret of success is to keep at it. The most effective exercises will do little to tone muscles and firm contours if abandoned after only a week or two. Set 20 minutes aside each day whenever you like, but never after a heavy meal. Once you have mastered the programme, repeat it twice a day rather than adding further repetitions indefinitely.

Start gently. The blue exercises are less demanding so concentrate on these to begin with if very unfit. When you get fitter, many exercises (particularly the red ones) can be made stronger by holding the positions. You may like to put more work in on particular weak points too. If slimming, be particularly conscientious with exercises for abdomen, buttocks and thighs.

These exercises are designed for relatively fit, healthy people. If you are not, check with your doctor before starting. If you have a knee condition, avoid vigorous kicking; if you have a chronic back condition, consult your specialist; if pregnant, avoid exercises on your front.

Bear two things in mind while exercising. The first is posture. Check you are standing, sitting or lying correctly before each exercise. If you are not holding yourself properly you may not be working the right muscles and joints. Pay attention to your breathing too. Always breathe out as you exercise — as you kick out or curl up or lean back — and in as you release the movement. Always finish exercising with at least 10 minutes complete relaxation, following instructions on page 108.

Exercise the muscles of your face by running through this routine. Start by crunching your face up into your nose, as though you have smelled something unpleasant (1). Then open your mouth and eyes as wide as you can (2) and stick your tongue out to release your throat muscles so that you are doing a silent 'scream' (3). This should be marvellously stimulating and relaxing. Proceed by pulling pursed lips to left (4) and right, and follow with a wide Cheshire-cat grin. Open your eyes wide and see if you can make the grin stretch from ear to ear. Hold, release and repeat, this time tucking in your chin and pulling your lower lip down as you do it. This will help firm the muscles at the front of your neck. Now run through the whole routine again.

facefacefac

1   2 3

Women seem to be particularly susceptible to tension in the neck and upper back. These stretching and loosening exercises will help persuade the tension to unlock. Use them whenever you are aware of any tightness there, and always start your exercising with this routine. Spend as long as you feel you need to on the sequence, as there is little point in working the rest of the body if the neck is tense and stiff. As you do these exercises bear in mind that your hands are there only to add weight and so increase the stretch and help with the exercise; they are not there to pull the head down. Pay attention to your body as you work and, if you feel the stretch is too strong, do the exercises without hands.

Use the second exercise (2 and 3) to see how tense you are. If very tense, the stretch you feel at the back of the neck will continue right down to the base of the spine. Either repeat the exercise until the tension eases or massage your neck with the palms and fingers of the hands, starting at the shoulder blades.

**Stretch up to ceiling (1), reaching as high as possible, several times.
Then clasp hands on back of head (2) and lower it slowly towards chest (3), until you feel stretch in back of neck. Hold and then release further. Come up slowly, breathing in.**

neckneckneck

Anchor one hand onto back leg of chair or stool, place other hand on head and let head drop diagonally forwards towards knee (4). Hold and release further into it when you can take more stretch. Repeat to other side. Now place hand on opposite side of head and lower it to side, bringing chin in and shoulders down (5). Feel stretch along side of neck. Repeat to other side.

4

5

6

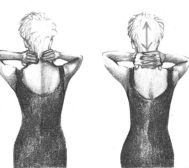

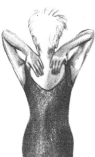

Clasp hands at back of head, press the head back and pull forwards with hands at same time (6). Place two thumbs just below the **base** of the skull so you can feel the neck muscles tighten. Hold for a moment, release and repeat.

Give yourself a neck massage. Stroke firmly upwards with hands and then knead the base of the neck. Finish by clasping hands together and pressing heels of hands firmly onto neck on either side. Release and then continue pressing, moving hands up and down, until tension eases...

The shoulders may be the most mobile joints of the body, but upper arms are a problem for many women. While no-one wants bulging muscles, the reverse — flab caused by slack muscles on the underside of the arm — also leaves much to be desired. Happily, this is one area where exercise can count for a great deal.

Make loose fists and hold both arms out as shown (1). Pull shoulder blades together, then press arms back several times. Rest and repeat, pressing arms upwards. Drop arms and circle shoulders backwards.

Strengthen upper arms. Make loose fists in front of you (2) and punch strongly back and upwards in firm movements, rotating arms inwards so back of hands face the front (3).

Lying on your back, using
0.5 kg (1 lb) weights, or food
cans, as here (4), pull arms
upwards to vertical (5) and
lower again. Repeat several
times slowly and then more
quickly. Finally, compensate
with a stretch in the opposite
direction. Clasp hands in
front, drop chin forwards,
round back and pull hands
away from you (6)...

armsarmsarms

You cannot separate your shape at the front from your shape at the back because each interacts with the other. Think of your spine as the frame around which the rest of you is constructed and adjust shape from there. Lower shoulders, lengthen spine, tuck buttocks under and you should notice an immediate improvement at the front. Further improvements can be achieved through diet and exercise. Both are important. While exercising can firm the waist in a matter of weeks, it will take longer at the hips, where underlying muscles are deeper.

There is a limit to how much exercise can firm the breasts because they are not muscles. But you can keep the underlying muscle toned, which will provide a firm base of support and so help prevent breasts sagging. Sit with arms crossed, as shown, and holding biceps firmly, press strongly inwards several times (3). Repeat at eye and waist levels in order to work every part of the muscle.

1

2

Firm waist: interlock fingers above head and bend to side, keeping shoulders down (1). Bend further with small successive movements and repeat to other side.

Twist to side and lower elbow towards knee (2), imagining a bar at your waist that you must lift over. Bend further as before and repeat to other side.

3

frontfrontfront

To firm abdomen, you need to work three major muscle groups, running vertically, horizontally and diagonally. Start by lying on your back, breathing out and curling up, bringing arms in front (4). Hold for two seconds (aim to build to slow count of five). As you get fitter, start with hands by sides then folded in front and, finally, wlth fingers interlocked behind head. Repeat this exercise to the sides to work the diagonal muscles (5), pulling well across body with top arm each time.

To help release the back after these strong exercises, let knees roll from side to side (6), so that the twist comes from waist and shoulders remain still. Finish by turning onto side and lifting both legs up together (7). Feel a tightening under your hand where horizontal abdominal muscles are contracting. Repeat slowly three times on each side.

Work shoulders and upper back by lying on floor with hands interlocked on bottom. Lift head and shoulders off mat as you pull hands downwards. Look up (1) and hold for a few moments. Lower head again and repeat several times. This is a marvellous corrective exercise for over-rounded upper back and shoulders. To strengthen lower back and firm buttocks: start with forehead on hands. Have legs hip-width apart. Bend legs (2), and slowly lift them alternately, up to six times if you can. Now place a cushion under your pelvis to take any strain off your lower back. Lift one leg, then the other, then lift both legs together (3) several times. Then describe wide circles in clockwise and anti-clockwise directions with both legs.

backbackback

Backs need careful looking after because they are susceptible to the strains of standing upright and soon weakened by poor posture and a sedentary lifestyle.

Exercises can help keep your back strong and supple by working the muscles that support the spine and encouraging the vertebrae themselves to move, but they must be bolstered by good posture all the time. 'Corrective' exercises for bad backs should only be done under strict supervision. If you have a previous history of back trouble, take these exercises gradually, starting with a bent leg and graduating to the more advanced ones when you feel that you have mastered the early exercises.

3

Discard cushion, rest a moment stretched out along the floor (4). Now stretch arms out and perform a 'diagonal arabesque' lifting alternate arms and legs off floor, looking up as you do so (5). Try to get the upper arm and thigh as far off the floor as possible. Lying in starting position (4), tighten buttocks and lift arms and legs off the floor simultaneously (6). Look up, hold for a few moments and lower. ALWAYS finish back work by curling up into a ball.

4

5

6

Exercise buttocks by sitting on a chair or stool, rounding the back and pressing thighs downwards so buttocks pull firmly together (7). Release and contract several times, slowly and quickly.

7

Exercise rather than diet will improve the shape of your legs for, while shedding extra weight may help, it is unlikely to make a significant difference unless you work at toning the muscles too. Here is a series of exercises that work all the major muscles of the upper leg, calves and ankles. Firm these up and you could be amazed at the difference. Also recommended: swimming, an excellent activity for streamlining and toning upper legs. Alternate vigorous crawl kick with backstroke.

Stand, holding onto a wall, and bend the knees (2). Bounce lightly up and down. Continue until you tire. This is an excellent pre-skiing exercise.

Firm front of thighs by sitting with hands on hips and back rounded. Flex foot, bend knee and kick out vigorously (1). Go on until the leg feels tired and well used. If your knee is weak, bend and stretch without kicking and skip the next exercise.

Strengthen ankles: sit with knees together and heels apart. Bring big toes together (3), trying to lift them up as much as possible. Then brush outwards along the floor again, pulling little toes upwards and pressing big toes down (4). Repeat until ankles and calves tire.

legslegslegs

Work outer thighs and hips by lying on side, with body and legs perfectly in line. Raise leg (5), keeping foot flexed and knee facing forwards. Do not aim for great height. Lower leg to half-way position (6) and raise again slowly.
Continue for at least 10 lifts. Feel it all the way from hip to outside of knee. Repeat to other side.

Stretch out muscle by standing, as shown (8) and, keeping knee in line with heel on forward foot, press your back heel down until you feel the stretch along back of calf. This is an extremely good warm-up exercise before running or jogging.

Firm inner thighs by lying, as shown, with a large cushion between the knees (7). Press firmly. Hold for a slow count of five before releasing. Repeat three times. Then do 10 quick squeezes.

Start with a salute to the day: a really big stretch, arms straight, feet hip-width apart (1). Stretch one arm up further, then the other, several times. Next, circle each arm backwards in wide circles to loosen shoulders. Follow by circling both arms together and then bend forwards from hip and swish arms through legs. Bend your knees as you do this if you have a weak back. Repeat three or four times, before returning to starting position. Extend arms out to sides and swing around, bending knee as you go (2) and focusing on something on a wall behind you. This will help prevent you getting dizzy. Repeat to other side and continue twisting from side to side until you feel really warmed up.

These body conditioners will exercise all major muscle groups, give heart and lungs a good workout too. But you should be relatively fit before starting. If you are not, practise the exercises on the previous pages every day for two weeks first…

The sequence should be fun. Familiarise yourself with the movements and establish a good rhythm, then add music. Always warm up into the jogging and wind down gradually afterwards, finishing with at least 10 minutes progressive relaxation, as outlined on page 108.

movemovemove

Reach up to ceiling (3) and bend to sides, keeping arms straight (4), so that you feel the stretch along your side, not in your back. Bend from side to side rhythmically several times. Now build a sequence, circling the body in one continuous movement. Bend (4), then twist into a diagonal forward stretch (5), continue down to brush past ankles (6), repeat diagonal stretch and side bend to other side and return to starting position stretching up. Make four circles each way, stretching as much as you can. Drop into 6 and swing loosely from side to side.

7   8

10

11

Whether inside in the gym or outside on the track, never stop exercising abruptly. Warm 'down' instead with these loosening exercises to keep joints supple and to prevent muscles from becoming stiff. Start with this 'rowing' sequence: sit on the floor with straight back, arms extended out to sides (10). Breathe in. Bend forwards towards feet and breathe out (the bend should come directly from the hip joint) (11). Breathe in and return to starting position. Breathe out as you round back and curl backwards with arms crossed over in front. Breathe in as you return to starting position.

94

9

Before you start jogging, do at least four deep knee bends, keeping heels on floor, to stretch out calf muscles. Begin by transferring your weight from foot to foot, lifting heels only (7). Continue by lifting and stretching each foot (8). Then jump from foot to foot, gradually lifting legs higher. Finally, place arms out in front (9), and bring thighs up to touch as you spring from foot to foot – without bringing hands down to meet them. Emphasize the upward spring and continue until comfortably out of breath.

Continue with series of straight leg kicks, starting on back and proceeding through the side (12) and front (13), before ending on the opposite side. Try to do 12 of each on each leg. To finish, curl up in a ball, breathe well and then relax, according to sequence on page 108.

12

13

nutrition

This profile should give an insight into how healthy your eating habits are. First, get an objective assessment. Compile a food diary, noting down *everything* you eat and drink over a two-week period.

Use a small notebook and fill it in immediately after eating. Include even the smallest snack. Now check your diet against the list of foods below.

Over the two-week period, did your diet include the following?
1. **Eggs** – at least three a week.
2. **Milk** – at least 275 ml (10 fl oz) whole or skimmed a day.
3. **Cheese** – at least 175 g (6 oz) a week.
4. **Offal, such as liver or kidney** – at least one serving a week.
5. **Meat or poultry** – at least four servings a week.
6. **Fish** – at least one serving a week.
7. **Seafood** – at least one serving in the two-week period.
8. **Vegetables** – at least two different types a day.
9. **Starchy carbohydrates** – wholemeal bread, cereal, potatoes, rice, pasta, pulses (at least two slices/helpings a day).
10. **Fresh fruit** – at least one or its juice a day.

There is a maximum score of 14 for each of the 10 food groups. For foods specified on a daily basis, score 1 point for each day on which these foods were eaten; for foods specified on a weekly basis, score 7 for <u>each</u> of the respective weeks; for seafood score 14. If you have an allergy to any of the foods, and cannot eat them, skip the offending category and award yourself 7. (If vegetarian, few of these groups will apply, so miss this section altogether.) Now add up your score.

<u>Maximum total score 133.</u> You should be able to gain top marks on this test very easily, but scores of over 115 still indicate that you eat in a healthy, varied way. Scores below this and, particularly, scores of less than 95, indicate that you should make some immediate alterations in your eating habits. If omitting some, or even most, of these foods from your diet, the chances are that you are eating too much highly refined and processed food. Rebalance your diet around these 10 essentials and omit, or at least cut down on, the rest. Read on for further guidelines on healthy eating.

Compiling a food diary is an excellent way of discovering what your eating patterns are. For example, do you tend to eat nothing most of the day and then eat one large meal? Or do you tend not to eat meals at all and to subsist on snatched snacks? Or is your appetite generally poor? Eating in a balanced way does not necessarily mean eating three conventional meals a day, but it does mean organising your eating timetable carefully so that your energy is sustained throughout it.

Healthy eating is enjoyable eating — the enjoyment springing as much from a renewed sensitivity to natural tastes and flavours and a generally enhanced sense of wellbeing as from the reassurance of knowing that you are eating in a moderate, balanced and nutritious way. Does this describe the way you eat, or do your eating habits and attitudes require revision? The basics of good nutrition can be summed up as follows.

1. **Make sure you get good quality protein – not necessarily meat. One meat meal a day is now recognized to be more than adequate. Find alternative sources in grains, pulses, nuts, dairy foods...**
2. **Reduce the overall amount of fat in the diet, replacing some animal fat with vegetable. If necessary, revise cooking methods (grill rather than fry); eat less red meat, more poultry and fish; eggs, butter, cheese and cream in moderation.**
3. **Eat plenty of fresh fruit and vegetables, preferably raw or very briefly cooked.**
4. **Cut out most refined flour and replace with wholegrains. Wholewheat bread is especially recommended and two slices a day is a healthy addition to any diet, whether slimming or not.**
5. **Make sure you are eating enough fibre – but not just adding bran for good measure (it inhibits absorption of essential minerals, calcium, iron and zinc). See list for some suggestions...**
6. **Cut out refined sugar.**
7. **Eat less salt.**
8. **Drink plenty of water. Watch intake of coffee, tea, cola, refined soft drinks and alcohol.**
9. **Balance food intake over the day.**
10. **Enjoy your food. Don't become too obsessive about vitamins, minerals and calories – simply be aware of how much better you feel on a healthy diet.**

If present eating habits are way off these 10 basics, be realistic. Do not expect to change everything overnight. Give yourself a month to relinquish bad habits, adopt better ones — and to lose some weight if necessary. Once you have overhauled your diet, make out a food diary again and check progress by comparing your score.

Approximate components of weekly diet

Food	Times eaten
Eggs	3-7
Liver	1-2
Fish	3
Meat	5
Poultry	2-3
Raw vegetables	12
Cooked vegetables	7
Fruit (raw and cooked)	18
Cheese	4-5
Yoghurt	3-7

% Fibre in foods

Bread and flour

Bread (white)	2.7
Bread (wholemeal)	8.5
Crispbread (rye)	11.7
Flour (plain white)	3.4
Flour (100% wholemeal)	9.6
Oatmeal	7
Wheat bran	44

Cereal

All Bran	26.7
Cornflakes	11
Muesli	7.4

Vegetables, fruit, nuts

Cabbage	2.8
Carrots	2.9
French beans	3.2
Haricot beans	7.4
Potatoes (baked with skin)	2
Apples	2
Apricots (raw)	2.1
(dried)	24
Brazil nuts	9
Dates	8.7
Desiccated coconut	24
Figs (raw)	2.5
(dried)	18.5
Lemon juice	0
Lemons, whole	5.2
Prunes	16.1
Raisins	6.8

There is considerable disagreement about how much of a particular mineral or vitamin you need. The UK's recommended daily requirement for vitamin C (30 mg), for example, has been doubled by the USA and almost doubled again by the Soviet Union, who recognize that there is a large divide between getting enough to protect against the deficiency diseases and getting enough for good health. Early signs of depleted vitamin or mineral levels constitute the all-too-familiar signs of poor health – dandruff, rough dry, scaly skin, bleeding gums, weak decaying teeth, fatigue, irritability, bloodshot eyes, styes, brittle finger nails and a lowered resistance to viruses and other types of infection. If any of these apply look first to your diet not to vitamin or to mineral supplements. You cannot transform a poor diet into a good one simply by sprinkling on a few vitamins or minerals. A broad spectrum daily multi-vitamin and mineral tablet can nevertheless act as a wise insurance against depleted levels caused by intensive farming methods and atmospheric pollution.

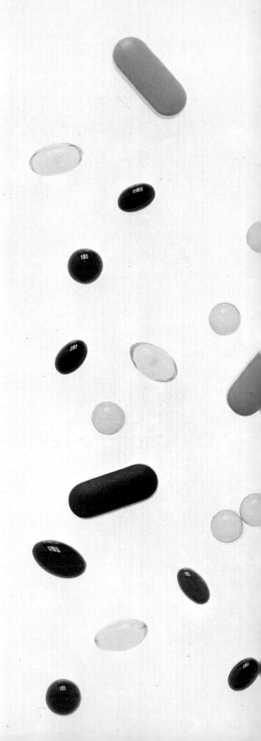

ABCDEFK

Slimming: do you need to examine your attitudes before embarking on yet another diet?

1. How often do you diet?
a) never **b)** rarely **c)** sometimes **d)** usually **e)** always

2. What is the maximum amount of weight that you have ever lost in one month?
a) 0-1,8 kg (0-4 lb) **b)** 1.9-4 kg (4.1-9 lb) **c)** 4.1-6.3 kg (9.1-14 lb)
d) 6.4-8.9 kg (14.1-19.9 lb) **e)** 9 kg or more (20 lb or more)

3. What is the maximum amount of weight that you have ever gained in a week?
a) 0-0.5 kg (0-1 lb) **b)** 0.6-1 kg (1.1-2 lb) **c)** 1.1-1.3 kg (2.1-3 lb)
d) 1.4-2.2 kg (3.1-5 lb) **e)** 2.3 kg or more (5.1 lb or more)

4. In a typical week, how much does your weight fluctuate?
a) 0-0.5 kg (0.-1 lb) **b)** 0.6-1 kg (1.1-2 lb) **c)** 1.1-1.3 kg (2.1-3 lb)
d) 1.4 2.2 kg (3.1-5 lb) **e)** 2.3 kg or more (5.1 lb or more)

5. Would a weight fluctuation of 2.2 kg (5 lb) affect the way you live your life?
a) not at all **b)** slightly **c)** moderately **d)** very much

6. Do you eat sensibly in front of others and binge alone?
a) never **b)** rarely **c)** often **d)** always

7. Do you give too much time and thought to food?
a) never **b)** rarely **c)** often **d)** always

8. Do you have feelings of guilt after over-eating?
a) never **b)** rarely **c)** often **d)** always

9. How conscious are you of what you are eating?
a) not at all **b)** slightly **c)** moderately **d)** extremely

10. How many pounds over your desired weight were you at your maximum weight?
a) 0-0.5 kg (0-1 lb) **b)** 0.6-2.2 kg (1.1-5 lb) **c)** 2.3-4.5 kg (5.1-10 lb)
d) 4.6-9 kg (10.1-20 lb) **e)** 9.1 kg or more (20.1 lb or more)

Score 1 for each **a** answer, 2 for each **b**, 3 for each **c**, 4 for each **d** and 5 for each **e**. Add them up. Out of a maximum of 45, scores of 30 or more indicate compulsive eating/dieting patterns; scores of between 12 and 30 a healthier outlook to eating and dieting; scores of less than 12 an almost total lack of concern with what you eat and weigh.

This balanced slimming diet provides about 1,200 calories a day, for a weight loss of about 1 kg (2 lb) a week

Breakfast 120 ml (4 fl oz) freshly squeezed fruit juice (see list opposite) OR half a grapefruit OR slice fresh pineapple OR wedge of melon.

1 egg, boiled or poached OR 20 g (¾ oz) unsweetened breakfast cereal OR 120 g (4 oz) porridge made with rolled oatmeal and water or milk from allowance.

1 piece of bread or toast with butter from allowance.

1 cup of coffee or tea (no sugar) with milk from allowance.

Mid-morning 1 cup of coffee or tea (no sugar) with milk from allowance.

Lunch (can be exchanged with Dinner).

One cup vegetable bouillon OR consommé OR fresh vegetable soup from the vegetables on list (boil, season, blend and add yoghurt from allowance or fresh or dried herbs for flavour).

Wholemeal sandwich made from two medium slices of bread, butter or margarine from allowance and 60 g (2 oz) chicken, lean ham, beef, turkey, salmon or tuna OR 30 g (1 oz) hard cheese. Add lettuce, watercress, tomato, endive, etc, as required.

Small salad made from listed vegetables with squeeze lemon juice and one piece fruit.

Mid-afternoon 1 cup of coffee or tea (no sugar) with milk from allowance.

Dinner (can be exchanged with Lunch).

120 ml (4 fl oz) vegetable juice from vegetables on list.

90 g (3 oz) chicken or lean meat OR 120 g (4 oz) steamed, baked or grilled (broiled) fish OR one two-egg omelette with chopped herbs (dill, parsley, basil, etc).

Salad OR any vegetable (steamed or boiled) from the list. One small baked potato OR one boiled potato (unpeeled) OR one tablespoon boiled rice.

One piece of fruit.

1 cup of coffee or tea (no sugar) with milk from allowance.

Allowances: 300 ml (10 fl oz) skimmed milk.
15 g (½ oz) butter or margarine.
1 carton plain, low-fat yoghurt.
Three cups of coffee or tea (without sugar).
As much water as you like (no alcohol).
7 eggs a week maximum.

Vegetables and fruit
EAT apples, asparagus, aubergine (eggplant), broccoli,
French, runner or string beans, Brussels sprouts, cabbage,
carrots, celery, chicory, all citrus fruits, courgette (zucchi-
ni), black, red and white currants, gooseberries, leeks,
lettuce, melon, mushrooms, onion, peaches, pears, pep-
pers, pineapple, plums, radishes, spinach, swede (ruta-
baga), tomatoes, turnips and turnip tops, watercress.

AVOID avocado pears, bananas, beetroot, broad
beans, haricot and lima beans, canned or frozen fruit or
vegetables (unless preserved without sugar), dried fruits
(dates, figs, apricots, raisins, etc), grapes, greengages,
lentils, nuts, parsnips, peas and sweetcorn (kernel corn).

Meat and fish
EAT lean beef, chicken, game birds (such as partridge,
pheasant or grouse), hare, lamb, offal (liver, kidney, heart,
brains), rabbit, turkey, veal, venison, most white fish (bass,
bluefish, catfish, cod, flounder, halibut, rockfish), salmon,
shellfish (clams, cockles, crab, lobster, mussels, oysters,
prawns, scallops and shrimps), sole.

AVOID bacon, canned meats and stews, corned beef,
duck, frankfurters, goose, luncheon meats, minced meat
(unless 100 per cent lean), mutton, rich pâtés, pork,
processed meats, salami, sausage, spare ribs. Fish canned in oil (i.e. tuna, salmon) unless well drained or
canned in their own juices, fish roes, herring, mackerel,
sardines.

dietsdietsdiets

lifestyle

Body and mind were once thought to be two quite separate entities. But now scientific research is showing they interact on a number of subtle levels. While negative emotions can increase susceptibility to stress, positive emotions and a healthy lifestyle seem to be able to protect. How fit are you for managing stress?

1. Do you smoke?

2. Do you drink more than five cups of tea or coffee a day?

3. Do you rely on sweet sugary things, such as soft drinks and chocolate, to keep you going?

4. Do you sleep badly?

5. On balance, do you work for more than nine hours a day?

6. Were you unable to take at least one complete day off last week?

7. Did you fail to take some type of exercise last week?

8. Are you more sensitive to criticism than you used to be?

9. Are you more irritable than you used to be?

10. Do you have difficulty in 'letting go' and laughing?

11. Do you suffer from: persistent mouth ulcers; digestive problems; outbreaks of dry, scaly skin; frequent headaches; nagging pain in the neck and lower back?

A score composed entirely or very largely of 'no' answers (9 or more) indicates that you are living in a healthy way that will minimize the potentially negative effects of other unrelated stresses that you do encounter. More than six 'yes' answers indicate that you are over-working, over-worrying and definitely increasing your chances of succumbing to stress-related ill health. Perhaps you already have (question 11).

Your lifestyle has as much to do with beauty as any of the more specific routines you may adopt. You can fast on orange juice for two days out of every seven, exercise frenetically from dawn to dusk, apply your make-up with scrupulous care but, if you do not know how to relax and how to enjoy the 'highs' and manage the 'lows' of life, you will never look or feel your best.

Find your optimum stress level by finding the stress that takes you up to, but not beyond, your limits — the point where you perform most efficiently, feel most stimulated and are at your happiest and most self-confident. Let stress rise above that level and you will feel agitated and unable to think or act clearly. Let it fall below it and you will feel bored, unfulfilled, drained of energy and enthusiasm.

If living below your optimum level, fend off boredom with variety and challenge. Seek new goals and interests. If living above it, modify your goals and take time off to pursue an activity that is enjoyable and creative — not competitive — and put the pressures of life aside for a while.

If you have 'Type A' personality traits — that is, you are highly competitive, ambitious and achievement-oriented — you should make a particularly determined effort to do this. US physicians Dr Ray Rosenman and Dr Meyer Friedman have shown a consistent link between this type of personality and stress-related ill-health — from tension headaches all the way through to complete physical and nervous breakdown.

How to control stress instead of letting it control you ...

Defuse stress by taking more exercise and practising some good relaxation techniques. Any type of stress alerts the body for physical action. If none follows, large amounts of hormones, such as adrenalin, together with their more dangerous by-products (such as free fatty acids which can raise cholesterol levels) are left circulating in the bloodstream with no chance of being burned off. Restore the balance. Remembering the old adage 'when in danger, when in doubt, shout and scream and run about', let off steam by taking more exercise. This is much more productive than politely suppressing your feelings or losing your temper and has another advantage too: by taking more exercise, you will be keeping

A confrontation at work, a tight deadline, the prospect of an evening out among strangers... There is no single definition of what makes one situation stressful and another not because the situation is not the major determining factor; the person is. Do you know what is stressful for you?

physically fit and experiments repeatedly show that healthy body makes for healthy mind... You can also defuse stress by practising the various relaxation methods outlined on the following pages.

Control the amount of change in your life. We all thrive on variety, but too much disorientates and may multiply the negative effects of other stresses you encounter ... take the big events in your life singly, not all at once.

Be single-minded. Although a certain amount of pressure can be beneficial because it channels thought and focuses the mind, too much pressure and too many conflicting demands on your time will lead to panic, confusion and an inability to think or act clearly. So be selective, decide what you are going to worry about and forget about the rest. No-one, however competent, can do more than one thing at a time — so focus your mind on the one thing that needs doing first, and do it ...

stressstress

The secret of relaxation is not to try too hard. It is a passive exercise not an active one. But the difficult art of doing less and less becomes even harder in a world where an ever increasing importance is placed on *doing* rather than *being*, on *making* rather than *letting* things happen. These relaxation and mind 'switching off' methods may help...

If, like many people, you find it difficult to relax, try these exercises and techniques and stick with the one that suits you best...

Progressive relaxation Lie on the floor with legs falling comfortably away from each other, arms away from your sides with palms facing the ceiling and head straight. Now stretch legs, pointing toes towards the floor as far as they will go. Hold the stretch and release, feeling the

tension gradually ebb away. Pull buttocks together, hold and release. Pull abdomen and pelvis into the floor, press hard and release. Stretch fingers out as wide as you can and release. Pull shoulders down away from ears and release. Open mouth wide in a 'silent scream' and release, letting mouth drop open and tongue lie flat. Swallow and feel your throat soften as the tension subsides. Take a deep breath, release your forehead and let go in a long drawn-out sigh...

Mind control Starting at the number 100, count backwards to zero, mouthing each number on the out-breath. Let your counting follow the rhythm of your breathing.

When other thoughts intervene, watch them passing across your mind, like a train travelling through a landscape, then return to your counting. As you get more practised, sequences will be longer, interruptions fewer and depth of relaxation greater...

Meditation You do not need a guru or even a particular philosophy to derive a great deal of benefit from meditation. Find 15 to 20 minutes when you know you will not be disturbed. Sit with legs crossed, hands folded in lap and back supported. Close your eyes and let your mind dwell on an object — a symbol, a rhythm of breathing, a phrase or word. Try the ancient Siddha yoga mantra *Om Namah Shivaya* or simply repeat the word *One* until your mind reaches a state of relaxed concentration. That's meditation.

Breathing Use breathing to quieten the mind and help you meditate. Sit as before with back straight and supported. Start by breathing out and count each breath until you reach 10. Focus only on your breathing. Although the technique sounds very simple, it is actually extraordinarily difficult. After two or three breaths, random thoughts will invariably rush in to distract you, forcing you to go back to the beginning and start all over again. However, with patience, you will find that concentration improves and, with it, inner peace.

Massage Massage is an excellent aid to relaxation (see next pages). A foot massage can be especially calming. Because many nerve endings lie in the sole of the foot the stimulating and soothing action of a foot massage can help restore equilibrium to body and mind. Try taking a small ball (a squash ball is ideal) and rolling it under your foot, varying the pressure as you go. Continue for at least three minutes, massaging every part of the foot from heel to toes. Does that side of your body feel different? Now repeat to other side.

Neck, shoulders and upper back are commonly tense. Release the tension by giving yourself a massage. Place an orange between you and a wall or door and roll it around by bending and straightening the knees. Concentrate on tense and painful areas – between the shoulder blades, along the spine, up across the shoulders and the neck... (This is not an exercise for smart walls, as the orange may stain.)

Body massage is one of the most pleasurable and practical ways of overcoming tension, reducing aches and pains and generating a powerful sense of wellbeing. Start with the basic strokes illustrated over the page and extend your repertoire as you become more proficient.

First of all, ask your subject to have a warm bath. Heat persuades muscles into a state of relaxed submission and so increases the benefits of the massage. Next, check you are both comfortable — a table at hip-height is ideal — and that there are as few outside distractions as possible. When your subject is lying on her front, place a pillow under the stomach to support lower back and a small cushion or folded towel under the forehead to support head and neck; when lying on her back, place a pillow under the knees.

Use a light oil to help your hands glide easily over the skin. Essential oils, diluted with a neutral oil such as wheatgerm, are perfect for this. Pour a small amount into your hands, rub them together to warm the oil and spread it over the surface on which you will be working. The back is always a good place to start, especially if you have never given a massage before because it's a large flat surface and often contains a great deal of muscular tension — particularly around neck and shoulders. Your hands should be supple and relaxed. Use them to communicate and your body to apply pressure and firmness, letting the movement come from your centre rather than just from wrists or elbows. You will then give a deeper, more even massage and — a plus — your arms will get much less tired. Massage only with the palms of the hands, fingers and pads of the thumbs. Applying pressure with elbows, knuckles or fists, as involved in some of the deep connective tissue massage techniques, should be left to the experts.

Your aim should be to establish a smooth working rhythm. Breathing evenly will help you achieve this. Breathe in as you move your hands over the body and out as you apply the pressure. As you become more practised you will become more sensitive to areas of tension in the body. Remember, muscle should feel quite spongy; if you feel a hard lump or knot along the muscle, the likelihood is that it is tense. Persuade tension to undo itself, either by massaging the entire length of the muscle or, if this is too tight and painful (as it will be if the muscle has gone into spasm), work gently but thoroughly around the area. You

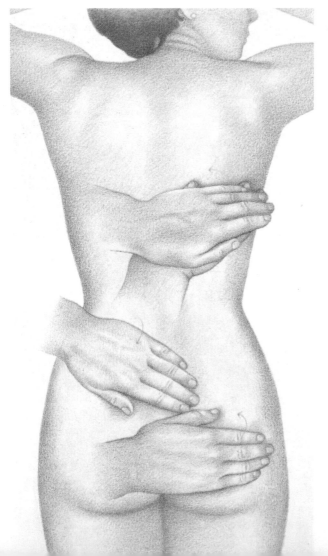

Start and end your massage with a simple long stroke of light to moderate pressure, massaging in the direction of the heart and gradually increasing pressure. A deeper stroke can be achieved by using the two hands together in differing circular directions, <u>left</u>, one going clockwise as the other goes anti-clockwise. Add pressure by clasping one hand on top of the other and travelling clockwise up one side, anti-clockwise up the other . . .

should find that the muscle unlocks as you release the surrounding tension.

Finally, bear in mind that massage should always be lighter over those parts of the body where the bone is near the surface — face, breast bone, lower rib cage (back and front), spine (hands move alongside not on top), hands, knees, calves and feet.

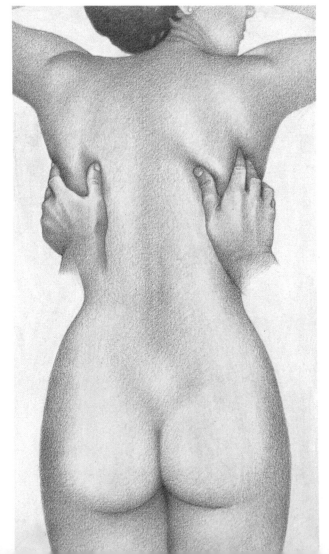

Kneading is excellent for relieving tension and is performed exactly as though kneading bread dough, with the pads of the fingers and thumbs, <u>left.</u> Friction (using the thumbs only) is excellent for releasing muscular spasm and can be used along entire length of spine, backs of calves, sides of ankles, heels and lower inside arms.

massage

Yoga

Yoga postures (*asanas*) are a practical way of counteracting stress and encouraging you to listen to your body and be aware of its needs. The straightforward steps here can be practised by anyone. Although some of the positions may appear awkward or difficult, they are not contortions and should be practised with gentle and precise movements — not with great athleticism. The postures are designed to refresh the body after an inactive day, increasing muscle tone and bringing oxygen to every cell in the body. Although they may appear to be static, you will soon discover that the spine and limbs will continue to stretch as the muscles relax. The postures can be held for some seconds, even minutes.

Jump feet about four feet apart and hold the arms out at shoulder level (3). Turn left foot in and right foot out, so that the whole leg turns outward from the hip. Aligning right heel with the middle of the arch of left foot, go into *virabhadrasana* II (warrior pose) (4). Bend knee (keeping it over the ankle and aiming, eventually, to form a right angle there) and stretch spine upwards. The weight should be evenly balanced. Repeat to other side.

Start by taking up *tadasana* (mountain pose) (1). Stand with heels and toes touching, toes spread as wide apart as possible. Pull up knees, tighten buttocks, stretch spine, drop and relax the shoulders. The chest will open as a result of the spinal stretching. Breathe evenly and deeply several times before taking up *vrksasana* (tree pose) (2). Point elbows out, press palms together, and rest foot on inner thigh. Relax into it, maintaining stretch in spine. Breathe evenly and deeply and remain there for as long as comfortable. Change legs.

Virasana (hero pose) Is performed keeping the knees together and sitting on the buttocks inside the feet. If the knees are weak, avoid this exercise; if the hips are stiff, use a cushion as shown (5). Place hands on soles of feet. If you find this difficult to do, sit in simple cross legs (6), interlocking the fingers for a more intense effect and stretching the arms up over the head. Finish with bharadvajrasana, a spinal twist. Bend the legs aside and keep the knees aligned with the hips (7). Rotate the trunk to face the outer thigh and catch the knee. Support the trunk with the other hand, stretch the spine and turn the head to look over the shoulder.

Health

This chart is for specific observations that will help you to understand how your body works over the course of both the 24-hour day, when vitality and alertness change with the clock, and the menstrual cycle, when fluctuating hormone levels may also affect your mood, energy and general wellbeing.

Key to filling in the chart

• The day of the month on which this chart begins is deliberately left blank so that you can start it immediately, whatever the date. Simply fill in today's date against day 1.

• Menstruation and ovulation. This is to enable you to see at a glance when your period is/was and to enter in the day when you think you have ovulated (see below). If you skip the temperature section, you can still get a rough indication of when you ovulated (though only in retrospect) by subtracting 14 days from the beginning of your period. When complete, look back over the chart to see how you felt.

• Temperature. There is no need to go through the rigmarole of taking your temperature every day unless you are using 'natural' methods of contraception (in which case you will also need skilled instruction, see next page), or you are trying to conceive. Take temperature first thing in the morning, while in bed and before you have had anything to eat or drink. Leave thermometer in your mouth for five minutes. Look for a slight dip in temperature (this does not always occur), followed by a rise of about 0.5°C (0.9°F). The dip indicates ovulation has just occurred; the rise that you are anywhere from a few hours to a few days past it (the rise continues for the rest of the cycle).

• Energy highs and lows. Simply place an H, M or L (high, medium or low) in the appropriate place, according to the time of day and how energetic you feel. We all have circadian rhythms – energy levels that rise and fall over the stages of a 24-hour day. While some of these peaks and troughs are so common as to apply generally (an example is the 1 pm lunch energy slump), others are more idiosyncratic.

• Symptoms. The symptoms involved here are mainly connected with the premenstrual syndrome. But the chart can be just as flexible as you want it to be. If you feel you have other symptoms that may be cycle-related, such as acne or compulsive eating, enter them.

• Suggested codes for symptoms: AB swollen, bloated abdomen (or ankles, wrists, fingers – specify); B breast tenderness; H headache; M migraine; S stomach pains; C clumsy; D depressed; I irritable.

Your daily and monthly rhythms

Day	Weight	Menst.	Ovul.	Temp.	Energy highs/lows morn.	noon	even.	sympt.

CONTRACEPTION: the alternatives

Method	Description
Combined oestrogen/ progestogen contraceptive pill (Effectiveness: 99.7%)	Alters hormonal behaviour, so that there is no 'true' menstrual cycle and the body is 'fooled' into thinking itself pregnant. It has four specific actions: 1. It prevents ovulation; 2. It reduced the 'motility' (muscular movement) of the Fallopian tube; 3. It prevents the thinning of the cervical mucus so that it remains sperm-resistant; 4. It prevents build-up of the womb lining.
Progesterone only pill (the "mini" pill) (Effectiveness with conscientious use: 98%)	This pill is taken daily throughout the cycle, even when menstruating, and must be taken at the same time each day.
Inter uterine device (IUD) or 'coil' (Effectiveness: 98.3%)	Copper-and-plastic or plastic only devices, fitted into the uterus with a loose thread so that you can check it is still in place. Copper devices release minute traces of the metal and are more effective.
Diaphragm or 'cap' (Effectiveness with conscientious use: 98%)	Blocks access of sperm to uterus. Must be used in conjunction with spermicide and left in place for six hours afterwards.
Condom (Effectiveness with conscientious use: 97%)	Rubber sheath that slips over the penis.
'Natural' contraception (Effectiveness with conscientious use: 85%)	A highly practical method (not the riskier rhythm method). Works by: 1. Assessing consistency of cervical mucus, which thins out just before ovulation. 2. Taking and charting your basal (resting) temperature over the menstrual cycle.
Sterilization (Effectiveness: approaching 100%)	Male sterilization (vasectomy) cuts or ties the *vas deferens*. Female sterilization destroys or blocks the Fallopian tubes.
Post-coital or 'morning after' contraception (Effectiveness: to be assessed)	Relatively high doses of oestrogen taken within 36 (preferably 12) hours and having an IUD fitted will prevent implantation of the fertilized egg in the uterus.

Drawbacks/Comments

In susceptible women, oestrogen may cause excessive blood clotting, which can lead to thrombosis, stroke or heart attack. Risk is highest in women over 35, especially if combined with smoking, overweight or high blood pressure.

In October 1983, two studies suggested links between cancer and the pill; the first breast cancer (due to high progestogen content) and the second cervical cancer. Although other studies have produced conflicting findings, women should give themselves regular monthly breast self-examinations (see page 122) and have cervical smears at intervals shown on Health Calendar over the page.

Higher incidence of breakthrough bleeding, irregular menstrual cycles and migraine in susceptible women.

The main advantage is the considerable lowering of the risk of blood clotting and, subsequently, thrombosis in high-risk women.

Painful heavy, prolonged periods plus an increased risk of anaemia, due to excessive loss of iron in the blood. Increased risk of pelvic infection.

Requires premeditation, motivation and can be messy.

May aggravate recurrent cystitis but reduces risk of cervical cancer.

Must be refitted after losing or gaining more than 4.5 kg (10 lb) in weight or after a pregnancy.

Loss of sensitivity for the man. High risk of pregnancy if sheath slips off or breaks during intercourse. Protects against venereal disease and cervical cancer.

A complicated method, at least initially, that requires motivation and specialized instruction at a 'natural' family planning clinic. As more accurate ways of identifying the fertile period are developed, this method is likely to become increasingly popular.

Any of the risks of normal surgery applies here, plus an increased risk of pelvic infection. When in doubt – DON'T. Numbers seeking reversal of sterilization are increasing.

Pills may produce nausea. The timing, dosage and right type of pills are essential. The IUD works within 60 hours and therefore makes a better 'late' choice than the course of oestrogens.

Screening is controversial. Some doctors consider it very helpful, potentially life-saving and too little practised, while others consider it a potential disservice because it may either engender unnecessary alarm or a false sense of security, even complacency, by encouraging people to hand the responsibility for their health over to their doctors. Your family history and your lifestyle – your diet, your smoking and drinking habits, and how much exercise you take – may be more important in determining good health than are regular check-ups, but infections and diseases can strike the healthiest individual. Happily, some of these can now be caught early enough to increase the prospects of successful treatment quite considerably. This more than justifies screening for them. The thinking on health checks has changed over the last decade or so. No longer is the annual 'physical' the preventative prescription. It is more important to have specific tests for 'high-risk' parts – breasts, cervix, heart – as age, sex and family history indicate. Use this chart to see at a glance which health checks you should be having when.

HEALTH CALENDAR: the whys and whens of screening

What?	When?
Complete physical check-up	Every two years from the age of 35 to the age of 50; annually after that.
Breast self-examination	Every month just after your period has finished; on the first day of each calendar month, if through menopause.
Mammography (minimal dose radiation)	Once at the age of 35 and annually thereafter. If 'higher' risk category, your doctor may suggest mammograms are ta earlier and/or more frequently.
Cervical smear	Soon after the time of first intercourse and again one year later; every three years up age 35 and every five years thereafter. Annually if history of herpes.
Blood pressure reading	Every three years up to age 35 and annua thereafter; annually whatever your age, i you smoke, are very overweight or have diabetes; when you are pregnant; whene your prescription for the contraceptive pi renewed.
Electrocardiogram (ECG) and blood/cholesterol reading	At age 35 in men; 40 for women; then as recommended – usually annually for men and less often for women. Your blood/cholesterol levels should be screened more frequently if past the menopause, a heavy smoker, take the Pill or substantially overweight.
Dental check-up and/or visit to dental hygienist	Teeth and gums should be checked every months and at the beginning of pregnan unless your dentist specifies otherwise. Have teeth scaled and professionally cleaned at least once a year.
Sight testing	At nursery school age (four or five); thereafter if problems present themselve Most people will require a sight test at between 40 and 50, combined with investigation for signs of cataract.

To establish that you are fit and in good health with no obvious or incipient signs of illness, that your lifestyle is healthy and that you have no risk factors, such as high blood pressure, that may lead to ill health.

To check for any changes in the breasts (see following page) that should be referred to your doctor for further investigation.

To give the doctor a 'baseline' reading of the normal architecture of the breast, if it is the first mammogram, against which subsequent X-rays can be referred to detect any changes; to pick up the 'high risk' breast — certain tissue patterns being linked with a higher incidence of cancer; to provide reassurance that all is well.

To detect the presence of abnormal cells on the cervix which may be pre-malignant (i.e. indicative of future cancer) and which, once found, can almost always be completely eradicated.

To check for high blood pressure (hypertension) which can be completely symptomless. It is important that you get your blood pressure checked regularly over the age of 35 (pressure tends to rise with age) because it is a recognized risk factor in heart disease (pumping against the high pressure places additional demands on the heart). A good average pressure is considered to be 120/80. Lower than average pressure is hardly ever a problem — and can be a health plus.

The ECG is considered of limited value for healthy people, but nevertheless important for getting a baseline pattern against which any subsequent deviations can be spotted. Of potentially greater value, however, is the blood/cholesterol test as raised levels are a recognized risk factor in coronary heart disease.

To check for early signs of tooth decay and/or gum disease. The visit to the hygienist is important because tartar (an accumulation of plaque) calcifies and hardens on the tooth and can initiate gum disease.

To check for long- or short-sightedness; to fit reading glasses to counteract the long sightedness that increases with age; to look for early signs of cataract.

Start with a visual inspection. Stand in front of a large mirror with a good light placed to the side, not overhead. Now look at your breasts. If this is the first time you have carried out a breast examination, take the opportunity to note exactly how they look.

To help check the differences between the two breasts, place the hands on top of the head and turn slowly to the left and the right. The crossways angle of the lighting should help you to spot any irregularities or dimpling in the skin surface.

BREAST SELF-EXAMINATION

Most breasts are naturally asymmetrical. Study your own carefully. As the key to breast examination is change, you must be aware of what is normal for you.

What to watch out for

- A lump. Probably less than 10 per cent of all lumps are cancerous, but it is impossible to tell by feeling whether it is innocent or not. Only a doctor can decide.
- Any moles that have changed in size, shape or colour.
- Dimpling or puckering, an unusual prominence in the blood veins on either breast, or a retraction of the skin.
- Inverted nipples. If nipples have always been inverted you have no cause for concern. If the nipple has recently become inverted, further investigation is required.
- A discharge coming from one or both nipples. Check for this by looking inside your bra before carrying out your monthly self-examination.
- Enlarged or inflamed lymph glands. See a doctor if they do not subside after three weeks.

Place your hands on your hips and press firmly down and inwards. This should tighten the pectoral muscle and thus help you to spot any dimpling. Then, keeping your hands where they are, lean forwards from the hips, so that the breasts fall straight downwards, and inspect them head-on. Look particularly for any tautness in the skin tissue, any change in the way the nipple is pointing, and for a nipple that becomes inverted on leaning over but everts itself naturally as you stand up again.

Lie down on a firm surface and place a folded towel or pillow beneath the shoulder of the side you examine first. Feel each breast with your fingers, keeping them straight, but not tense. Pressure should be firm enough for the skin surface to move with your fingers but not so firm that the natural texture becomes hard and lumpy. Press the breast tissue towards the chest wall, starting just above the nipple and radiating outwards. Finally place your arms above your head and repeat examination, paying attention to the upper part of the breast which extends into the armpit.

Index

Acknowledgments

ILLUSTRATIONS

The Publishers would like to thank the following organisations and individuals for their kind permission to reproduce the photographs in this book:
Werner Forman Archive 4; Tim Graham 7; Alan Randall/Vogue 47; Albert Watson/Vogue 9, 16, 21.

The following photographs were taken specially for Octopus Books: Robert Golden 97, 102-3; Tim Simmons 105, 106-7; Charlie Stebbings 28-9, 99, 100-1.
All other photographs by Sandra Lousada.

Artwork by: Maire Smith and Martin Welch

TEXT
Page 75 Weight graph devised from weight/height tables produced by the British United Provident Association (BUPA) and reproduced with their permission.
Page 101 Compulsive eating/dieting questionnaire adapted from Internal and External Components of Emotionality in Restrained and Unrestrained Eaters devised by J. Polivy, C.P. Herman and S. Warsh in the *Journal of Abnormal Psychology*, 1978, 87, page 497.
Page 99 Fibre values for listed foods taken from McCance and Widdowson's *The Composition of Foods* by A.A. Paul and D.A.T. Southgate, published by Her Majesty's Stationery Office (London, 1978) and reproduced with the permission of The Controller Her Majesty's Stationery Office.
Page 11 Sun protector factor chart compiled from papers produced by Piz Buin Protective Tanning.
Pages 48-9 Face measurements based on material from Mademoiselle Magazine, U.S.A.